Poland 1939

The birth of Blitzkrieg

Campaign · 107

Poland 1939

The birth of Blitzkrieg

Steven J Zaloga · Illustrated by Howard Gerrard

Series editor Lee Johnson · Consultant editor David G Chandler

First published in Great Britain in 2002 by Osprey Publishing, Elms Court, Chapel Way, Botley, Oxford OX2 9LP, United Kingdom.
Email: info@ospreypublishing.com

CIP Data for this publication is available from the British Library

ISBN 1 84176 408 6

Editor: Lee Johnson
Design: The Black Spot
Index by Alison Worthington
Maps by The Map Studio
3D bird's-eye views by The Black Spot
Battlescene artwork by Howard Gerrard
Originated by Magnet Harlequin, Uxbridge, UK
Printed in China through World Print Ltd.

04 05 06 07 08 10 9 8 7 6 5 4

FOR A CATALOGUE OF ALL BOOKS PUBLISHED BY
OSPREY MILITARY AND AVIATION PLEASE CONTACT:

The Marketing Manager, Osprey Direct UK,
PO Box 140, Wellingborough, Northants,
NN8 2FA, United Kingdom.
Email: info@ospreydirect.co.uk

The Marketing Manager, Osprey Direct USA,
c/o MBI Publishing, PO Box 1,
729 Prospect Avenue, Osceola, WI 54020, USA.
Email: info@ospreydirectusa.com

www.ospreypublishing.com

Author's Note

The author would like to acknowledge his gratitude for the generous support and help of the noted Polish historian and writer the late Janusz Magnuski, as well as the hospitality of his wife, Magda Chomicz, on the many occasions when the author was in Warsaw on research. The author would also like to thank the staffs of several archives for their support over the years, including the Pilsudski Institute in New York, and the Sikorski Institute in London. Thanks go to the staffs of the Military History Institute at the US Army War College at Carlisle Barracks, and the US National Archives at College Park where the author conducted research on the German side of the campaign. Colonel David Glantz (US Army, ret'd) was, as always, very helpful in regards to the Soviet side of this campaign. Special thanks to Frank DeSisto and Josef Janik for help in obtaining several of the photos used here. Thanks also go to Dr Jack Atwater, director of the US Army Ordnance Museum at Aberdeen Proving Grounds, for his help photographing preserved Polish weapons from the museum collection.

Artist's Note

KEY TO MILITARY SYMBOLS

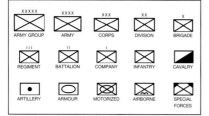

CONTENTS

INTRODUCTION

The German invasion of Poland on 1 September 1939 signalled the commencement of the Second World War. The outcome of the campaign was a foregone conclusion. It pitted the newly modernised army of Europe's greatest industrial power against the smaller army of its impoverished eastern neighbour. To further tip the scales, Germany had entered a pact with the Soviet Union before the start of the campaign, with the Red Army invading Poland two weeks after the start of the German attack. Polish strategy hinged on the entry of France and Britain into the war, but this provided no solace when the French army remained secure behind the Maginot line.

Even if the outcome of the Polish campaign was predictable, its nature was not. The 1939 campaign represented the first demonstration of a new style of warfare, popularly called 'Blitzkrieg'. The German armed forces blended the tactical lessons of the First World War with the new technologies of armoured vehicles, combat aircraft and radio communications to create a devastating new form of combined-arms warfare. The German assault was spearheaded by Panzer divisions whose firepower and shock was further amplified by the use of Stuka dive-bombers. The Polish army of 1939 was not as backward as is often portrayed, and its stubborn defence gave the Germans the occasional surprise, for example the Bzura counter-offensive. The German army had still not perfected its novel tactics, and German casualties were relatively heavy for such a short campaign. The Polish campaign proved to be a crucial learning experience for the Wehrmacht. It uncovered the shortcomings in German training and doctrine, and made it possible for the Wehrmacht to perfect Blitzkrieg prior to its greatest challenge – the assault on France in 1940.

If a single image dominates the popular perception of the Polish campaign of 1939, it is the scene of Polish cavalry bravely charging the Panzers with their lances. Like many other details of the campaign, it is a myth that was created by German wartime propaganda and perpetuated by sloppy scholarship. Yet such myths have also been embraced by the Poles themselves as symbols of their wartime gallantry, achieving a cultural resonance in spite of their variance with the historical record.

ORIGINS OF THE CAMPAIGN

Hitler's rise to power in Germany in the 1930s was nourished by Germany's deep sense of humiliation after her defeat in the First World War. The harsh settlement terms imposed by the Allies and the loss of former German territory in the east to the new states of Czechoslovakia and Poland was bitterly resented. These sentiments were effectively exploited by the Nazis in their rise to power. Tensions were further amplified by the fetid stew of Nazi racial ideology that linked the resurgence of the German nation with the violent seizure of *lebensraum* (living space) from the sub-human Slavs on Germany's eastern frontier.

Having rejected the demilitarisation of the German armed forces soon after taking power, by the late 1930s Hitler was ready to utilise Germany's growing military might to further his political ambitions. In September 1938, he pressured France and Britain to acquiesce to his seizure of the Sudetenland (the border areas of Czechoslovakia with the highest proportion of German population). The appeasement of Germany at the Munich conference in 1938 served as a catalyst to the ensuing war. It convinced Hitler that France and Britain were led by timid men who could be bluffed and bullied into further territorial concessions. It similarly convinced Stalin that France and Britain would not back their commitments to the security of the states of east-central Europe so, therefore, the Soviet Union would have to reach its own accord with Germany. As was the case with Germany, Russia had lost territory in the wake of the First World War to the new states of east-

The most enduring myth of the 1939 campaign has been the tale of Polish cavalry charges against German Panzers. Here, a Polish lancer regiment conducts exercises prior to the outbreak of the war. The lance had been dropped as a weapon before the war, but was still widely used in training. (Pilsudski Institute)

Animosity between Poland and Germany pre-dated the Hitler period. There was bitter fighting between Polish and German paramilitary formations from 1918 to 1922 over control of the border areas of Silesia and Pomerania, which had mixed German and Polish populations. The matter was settled by plebiscites in 1922, but Germany remained aggrieved over the loss of major cities like Posen (Poznan). This picture shows a Polish infantry unit during the 1922 fighting in Pomerania. (J. Janik)

central Europe and so shared a desire to rectify the existing territorial boundaries. While the two nations' Marxist and Nazi ideologies seemed diametrically opposed, the state interests of Germany and the Soviet Union converged in 1939.

The Munich concessions were hailed by the British prime minister of the time, Neville Chamberlain, as offering 'peace in our time', but by early 1939 the leaders of both Britain and France began to recognise that Hitler's territorial demands were insatiable. Instead of softening Paris and London into making further concessions, the Munich crisis led to a stiffening of Anglo-French resolve to finally confront the Nazi menace. The situation further deteriorated on 15 March 1939 when German troops seized the remainder of the Czech lands and formed a puppet Slovak state.

In late March 1939, Hitler informed the leaders of the German armed forces that the 'Polish question' would have to be solved by military means. Hitler used the lingering resentment over German territorial losses to Poland in 1918–22 as the pretext for war. The most significant irritant was the separation of East Prussia from the rest of Germany by the former German territory known as the Pomeranian corridor. In addition, the major German Baltic port of Danzig had been converted to a 'free city' to permit its use by both Poland and Germany. The Germans chafed over Polish control of the eastern areas of Pomerania and Silesia, which had been ceded to Poland in the early 1920s after a bitter civil war and an Allied-sponsored plebiscite.

Although these areas had a majority Polish population, there were substantial German minorities especially in the cities such as Poznan (Posen). In October 1938 Hitler began putting pressure on Poland to permit the creation of an extra-territorial road through the corridor to Prussia. He also wanted the reversion of Danzig to Germany. Hitler's two requests were followed by further diplomatic efforts in January and March 1939, the latter being met by a partial Polish mobilisation.

Through most of the 1920s, Poland's strategic plans had hinged on its alliances with France. Paris had attempted to create a strategic grouping of allied states in east-central Europe as a bulwark against German or Soviet expansion. By the 1930s, the 'little entente' was falling apart. From a strategic point of view, its greatest failure was the inability of the Polish and Czechoslovak governments to overlook their minor territorial disputes and form a military alliance against Germany. By 1939, it was too late.

Warsaw responded negatively to the German diplomatic moves of 1938–39, assuming quite rightly that they were merely pretexts for German territorial aggrandisement at Poland's expense. After the cession of the Sudetenland to Germany in 1938, Warsaw was concerned that Germany would attempt similar diplomatic tactics against Poland in an effort to gain control of the corridor, Danzig and some of its western territories. French influence was on the wane in the region, and on 31 March 1939, the British government announced its guarantee of Polish security, including maintaining the status quo of Danzig.

The Soviet Union had been excluded from these discussions, largely due to the understandable Polish fear that any Soviet military intervention in the region would be tantamount to eventual occupation. Although both Britain and France were interested in involving Moscow in an anti-German coalition, they could not overcome Warsaw's suspicions about long-term Soviet aims in the region. As a result of German diplomatic successes in 1938 and 1939 and the apparent vacillation and weakness of France and Britain, Stalin began to consider a possible treaty with Germany. Stalin had his own territorial ambitions in the region, and so long as Germany was going to seize territory, he decided to follow suit. Much of the eastern half of Poland had been under Russian control from the partitions of the 18th century until 1918, and the significant presence of Byelorussians and Ukrainians in the region provided the pretext for territorial absorption. In addition, Stalin was interested in regaining control of other former Tsarist imperial territories including the Baltic states, Moldova and parts of Finland. In the summer of 1939, the German ambassador in Moscow began informal talks with the Soviet government about a possible treaty. The announcement on 25 August 1939 by foreign ministers Ribbentrop and Molotov that Germany and the Soviet Union had signed a non-aggression pact stunned the world, since few believed that these two erstwhile ideological adversaries would ever join forces. For both Hitler and Stalin it was a temporary marriage of convenience as would become apparent two summers later.

The Ribbentrop–Molotov pact gave Hitler the green light for the invasion of Poland. Hitler was convinced that he, and he alone, was the genuine representative of the will of the German people and, therefore, the best suited to rally the nation for war. He was convinced that the

Adolf Hitler was the primary architect of the plan to go to war with Poland. The senior leadership was far more hesitant about the plans for war, rightly fearing that the war would broaden into a conflict with the powerful alliance of France and Britain. Hitler was dismissive of the willingness of France and Britain to enter the war over Poland. Here, Hitler receives a briefing on operations in Poland from Wilhelm Keitel, the head of the OKW armed forces high command. (NARA)

weak leaders of Britain and France would try to avoid war at all costs, and that even if there were a response to the invasion, it would be weak and indecisive. The ultimate contest would be with the victors of the First World War, France and Britain, but before that conflict the Wehrmacht had to prove itself in battle. Poland presented an ideal opportunity since its unfortunate strategic position between Germany and the Soviet Union ensured its destruction. On 23 August 1939, Hitler addressed the commanders of the German armed forces and outlined his objectives in the war with Poland. The date for invasion was initially set as 26 August 1939, but Hitler hesitated when Britain pledged military support to Poland. Last-minute diplomatic efforts were put in motion to further discredit the Polish government in world opinion by portraying the legitimacy of the German demands and the obstinacy of the Poles. A border violation was cooked up to provide an excuse for invasion. While these diplomatic shenanigans were taking place, the German commanders warned Hitler that their forces could not be indefinitely held at their jumping-off points without losing the element of surprise. As a result, on 31 August 1939, Hitler ordered the invasion to begin the following day.

CHRONOLOGY

1938

29 September Britain and France agree to German demands that Czechoslovakia cede the Sudetenland at the Munich conference,

1–7 October German troops occupy the Sudetenland in Czechoslovakia

1939

15 March German army invades the remainder of Czechoslovakia, occupies Bohemia–Moravia and eventually allows Slovakia to form puppet state

22 March Germany seizes port of Memel from Lithuania

25 March Hitler orders start of preparations to invade Poland

March Polish army begins partial mobilisation in response to German diplomatic pressure to cede Pomeranian corridor and allow return of Danzig to Germany

31 March British government announces its guarantee of Polish security, including maintaining the status quo of Danzig

May Polish and French general staff hold meetings in France, during which France pledges major offensive against Germany two weeks after an invasion

23 August German foreign minister Ribbentrop and Soviet foreign minister Molotov announce German–Soviet non-aggression pact; which includes secret clauses agreeing to the dismemberment of Poland

24 August Britain gives written assurances to Poland in the event of war with Germany

26 August Hitler planned to start war today, but postpones the attack in wake of British security announcement

1 September War begins at 0400hrs with German battleship *Schleswig-Holstein* firing at Polish garrison on Westerplatte near Danzig

2 September German advances out of East Prussia force Army Modlin to withdraw to Vistula line

3 September France and Britain declare war on Germany

5 September Piotrkow falls, and the gateway to Warsaw is opened to German Panzers; in the evening, Armies Lodz, Krakow, Prusy and Poznan ordered to begin retreat behind the Vistula

7 September German tanks reach outskirts of Warsaw, but are thrown back in intense street fighting. Marshal Rydz-Smigly decides to shift headquarters from Warsaw to Brzesc-nad-Bugiem

9 September Army Poznan launches counter-attack along the Bzura River, catching the German 8th Army off guard

15 September Army Group North reaches northern outskirts of Warsaw, siege resumes

16 September Polish forces along the Bzura subjected to massive artillery and air attack; retreat to Warsaw ordered that evening

17 September Red Army begins to invade Poland from the east

19 September Army Krakow attempts to break out towards Romania through Tomaszow Lubelski

21 September Last units from Bzura counter-offensive finally surrender

22 September Encircled by German and Soviet troops, city of Lwow finally surrenders

25 September 'Black Monday', a massive Luftwaffe attack on Warsaw causes heavy civilian casualties

26 September Southern Warsaw forts captured

27 September Warsaw garrison surrenders

29 September Fortified Modlin garrison surrenders

6 October Battlegroup under General Franciszek Kleeberg surrenders after a four-day battle around Kock; last major Polish unit in the field

OPPOSING COMMANDERS

Field Marshal Wilhelm Keitel was appointed head of the OKW in 1938. Although he had hopes to establish the OKW as a unified command over all armed forces, Goering's important role with the Luftwaffe limited the amount of control the OKW could exercise over the air arm. (NARA)

GERMAN COMMANDERS

The choice between peace and war was clearly down to **Adolf Hitler**. The Führer usurped the control of grand strategy from the German High Command (OKH) even before the war began. He forced the resignation of the chief of the general staff, Ludwik Beck, in August 1938, when his lack of confidence in Hitler's belligerent schemes became apparent. While few generals were opposed to war against a traditional enemy like Poland, the senior leadership of the Wehrmacht was not enthusiastic for the campaign, fearing that it would precipitate a war with France and Britain. Most German military leaders at the time thought that the Wehrmacht was not yet ready for war with the Western powers. Hitler's success at Munich in 1938 gave him greater credibility, but mistrust remained between the Führer and the senior leadership through 1939. The generals' ambivalence towards Hitler's war plans would later be thrown in their faces after the spectacular victory over France in 1940, which would also help create the mystique of Hitler's strategic genius for war.

Later in the war, Hitler would take a more direct role in the conduct of German operations. In the case of the Polish campaign he played a more traditional role as supreme political leader, leaving the planning for the fighting up to the officer corps. Germany's military leadership was well respected for its professionalism and training. In spite of prohibitions in the Versailles treaty, Hans von Seeckt re-established a clandestine general staff system in 1920. Most of the senior leaders of 1939 had fought in the First World War and were handpicked by Seeckt to serve in the rump Reichswehr after the war. The limitations imposed by the Allies under the Versailles treaty did not deter the Reichswehr from developing innovative new tactics and doctrine; applying the lessons of the recent conflict to the likely shape of future wars. These studies were far more rigorous than elsewhere in Europe. As losers in the last conflict, the Germans had fewer sacred cows to defend.

The Reichswehr and the Wehrmacht managed to institutionalise the development of superior military leaders, especially at the operational and tactical level of war. The professional focus of German officer training led to a limited comprehension and even disdain for economic and political issues, which led to a far weaker appreciation of war and logistics at a strategic level. These shortcomings were not manifest in the first year of the conflict, but they would have important repercussions later in the war.

The senior ranks of the army were ambivalent towards Hitler. On the one hand, they rejoiced at his avid support of the military, his rejection of the restrictions of the Versailles treaty and his rejuvenation of

ABOVE **Field Marshal Walter von Brauchitsch was commander-in-chief of the German army during its most spectacular victories of 1939–41. He was relieved of command by Hitler in December 1941 after the campaign in the Soviet Union had bogged down. (NARA)**

RIGHT, TOP **Generaloberst Franz Halder headed the general staff during the Polish campaign, but delegated much of the work on the attack plan to his subordinates. (NARA)**

RIGHT, BOTTOM **Generaloberst Gerd von Rundstedt was the most important German field commander of the Polish campaign. He not only played a central role in the development of the Case White plan, but also led the most important field command in the fighting, Army Group South. (NARA)**

German national pride. On the other hand, most were from aristocratic families with traditional conservative or authoritarian politics and, therefore, disdainful of the Nazi upstarts and their radical views. Hitler, the former corporal, attempted to usurp aspects of war planning that had previously been the preserve of the senior military. There were even some half-hearted schemes for a conservative army coup against Hitler; but these were never credible as Seeckt had installed in the officer corps the belief that obedience to the state was their honour. Younger officers were more attuned to Hitler's schemes, all the more so as Germany scored victory after victory in the late 1930s at little or no cost. Hitler proved to be an able politician, manipulating the senior leadership of the army by installing pliable officers in the senior staff positions. He also ensured the loyalty of his field commanders by exploiting their sense of duty to Germany. The crises of 1938 led to considerable turmoil in the ranks of the senior army leaders.

Prior to the outbreak of war, Hitler abolished the old War Ministry and assumed the position of commander in chief. The Oberkommando der Wehrmacht (OKW), the armed forces high command, replaced the war ministry. The head of the OKW was **Wilhelm Keitel**. Like so many other senior German staff officers in the Second World War, Keitel had been an artillery officer in the First World War at a time when artillery was the dominant branch of service. After being wounded in 1914, his abilities brought him to the attention of the general staff, on which he served for the remainder of the war. Keitel replaced the former war minister, Werner von Blomberg, in 1938 following a personal scandal that led to his downfall. Keitel's new position was largely administrative and his quest for a unified command of the armed forces never coalesced, as control of the Luftwaffe remained in the hands of one of Hitler's cronies, Hermann Goering.

Keitel was ably served by **Alfred Jodl**, chief of the operations office. Jodl, like Keitel, had served in the artillery in the First World War, and his abilities led to his appointment to the clandestine general staff after the war. He rose quickly in the interwar army, and assumed his post on the OKW staff after his predecessor, Max von Veibahn, suffered a nervous breakdown during the Austrian annexation in 1938. As war approached, Jodl attempted to secure a divisional command, but in August 1939 he was brought back to the OKW by Keitel. Nevertheless, the key planning for the Polish operation fell to the army, not the OKW.

ABOVE **Generaloberst Fedor von Bock commanded the other major field formation of the Wehrmacht in the 1939 campaign, Army Group North, which was responsible for sealing the Pomeranian corridor and attacking Warsaw from East Prussia. (NARA)**

ABOVE RIGHT **General Johannes Blaskowitz commanded the Tenth Army during the campaign, Rundstedt's 'problem child'. Typical of the older and more traditional German generals, Blaskowitz protested the violence and lack of discipline of SS units in Poland, which isolated him from Hitler's inner circle as the army became Nazified during the war. (NARA)**

The army's commander in chief (Oberkommando des Heeres, OKH) was **Feldmarshal Walter von Brauchitsch**, a Silesian aristocrat who had served as a staff officer in the First World War and received the Iron Cross. Although not an avid Nazi, he was indebted to the Nazi party financially and for keeping secret the more sordid aspects of his messy divorce and remarriage. Suitably compromised, he offered no resistance to Hitler's plans even if he had personal doubts about their wisdom. The chief of the general staff was **Generaloberst Franz Halder**, who had replaced Ludwik Beck in the midst of the Czech crisis in 1938. Under Hitler, the general staff no longer had the influence it had during the days of Moltke and Schlieffen in Germany's two previous wars. Halder, who was a monarchist and a practising Christian, was another Prussian general with little personal enthusiasm for the Nazis. He was regarded by other German generals as a competent if mediocre commander. He accepted his position with some reluctance, feeling that a more ardent supporter of the Nazis, such as Erich von Manstein, would have been a better choice. But Brauchitsch had encountered difficulties working with Manstein in the past and convinced Halder to accept. Once at his post, Halder took up his assignment with enthusiasm and brought together a superb team under Generaloberst Gerd von Rundstedt to plan the Polish operation.

Field command of the German army in the Polish campaign was split between Army Groups North and South. **GenObst Gerd von Rundstedt**, who helped plan the campaign, commanded the larger of the two forces, Army Group South, with Generalleutnant Erich von Manstein as his chief of staff. Rundstedt, who was from an aristocratic Prussian military family, had a distinguished career during the First World War, rising from an infantry company commander to corps chief of staff. His service under the influential Hans von Seeckt ensured him a position in the interwar army. Rundstedt lacked interest in political affairs, but his skills catapulted him into senior command positions both under the Weimar Republic and Hitler's Third Reich.

Army Group North was commanded by **Generaloberst Fedor von Bock**, whose career had parallels to Rundstedt's. Both men were among the five young staff majors advanced to lieutenant-colonelcies by Seeckt in October 1920 to form the core of the new clandestine general staff. Von Bock also enjoyed a brilliant career through the interwar years; testament to Seeckt's judgement. A third of the young majors, **Ritter von Leeb**, commanded Army Group West, which controlled forces facing France during the Polish campaign.

POLISH COMMANDERS

The singular influence on Poland's commanders was the legacy of **Josef Pilsudski**, the leader of Poland until his death in 1935. Pilsudski was a

ABOVE **Marshal Eduard Rydz-Smigly was the Polish commander and chief in the 1939 campaign. One of Pilsudski's most able field commanders in the 1920 Russo-Polish war, Rydz-Smigly's leadership in the hopeless campaign of 1939 led to bitter recriminations after the war. (Pilsudski Institute)**

ABOVE, RIGHT **General Kazimierz Sosnkowski was Rydz-Smigly's main rival for the command of the army after Pilsudski's death. He commanded the Southern Front in the final weeks of the campaign, and later headed the Polish armed forces in exile in Britain. (J. Janik)**

RIGHT **General Stefan Dab-Biernacki commanded the main strategic reserve, Army Prusy, in the opening weeks of the campaign. He was then assigned to command the ill-fated Northern Front. He had commanded the 1st Division of Pilsudski's Legion during the wars for independence of 1917–20. (J. Janik)**

socialist politician whose elder brother had died on the Russian gallows alongside Lenin's brother for revolutionary activities against the Tsar. At the outbreak of the First World War, Pilsudski attempted to entice the Austro-Hungarian government to support the formation of Polish military units to fight the Russians. Concerned over separatist nationalism in the empire, the Austrians showed little enthusiasm and threw Pilsudski in prison. But Pilsudski's Legion attracted a score of avid young nationalists, many of whom would later become key military leaders. The collapse of the Russian and Austro-Hungarian empires and Germany's defeat permitted the recreation of an independent Polish state 123 years after it had last been partitioned by its neighbours. Poland's independence, although sanctioned by the Western powers, had to be secured by force of arms. The most serious of these conflicts was the war between Poland and Bolshevik Russia in 1919–20. Pilsudski's inspired leadership during the war both as a national figurehead and military commander led most Poles to regard him as the saviour of the nation. Pilsudski withdrew from public life after the war, though he remained influential in army affairs. To the relief of many, Poland's fractious and embarrassing experiment in democracy came to a halt in 1926 with Pilsudski's bloodless seizure of power. Pilsudski became the power behind the throne, aloof from the day-to-day workings of the government, but in control of important aspects of political life. His death in 1935 left the country adrift, as his successor, General Edward Rydz-Smigly, was ill-prepared to fill the shoes of so charismatic and talented a leader.

The new Polish army of the 1920s had to be created from scratch. Those officers with military experience had served in three different armies: German, Austro-Hungarian and Tsarist Russian, all with different military traditions and training. As a result of their long tradition of nationalist uprising, few Poles were trusted in senior command positions in the imperial armies. A cadre of officers had been trained in France in 1918, and those with the legions had informal training at best. Pilsudski was generally successful in moulding these disparate strands into a cohesive officer corps. With France as Poland's principal ally in the 1920s, many Polish staff officers received their advanced training in French academies. Staff academies were established in Warsaw based on the French model, and this has often left military historians with the impression that Polish defence planning was shaped by French doctrine. However, this was not the case, as the Polish experience of war in 1918–22

General Tadeusz Kutrzeba had been involved in the development of Plan West, the Polish defensive scheme in 1939. As commander of Army Poznan, he was instrumental in planning and leading the Bzura counter-offensive.

was completely different from the trench fighting in 1914–18. While the French military culture stressed the need for methodical battle, the Polish tradition, strongly influenced by Pilsudski himself, stressed improvisation. By 1939 the Polish army had developed a competent general staff and the French attaché deemed that their war planning was very professional, indeed 'almost French'.

Marshal Edward Rydz-Smigly headed the General Inspectorate of the Armed Forces (GISZ), which had been created by Pilsudski in the late 1920s to control the armed forces instead of the general staff. Rydz-Smigly had joined Pilsudski's paramilitary forces prior to the First World War, and he headed the clandestine military forces after Pilsudski was thrown in jail. He was one of Pilsudski's most talented and trusted field commanders, leading the Polish units that seized Wilno (in the summer of 1919), Dunaberg (in Latvia later in 1919) and Kiev (in Ukraine in 1920). During the defence of Poland against the Bolsheviks in 1920, Pilsudski entrusted Rydz-Smigly with the defence of Warsaw and the later campaign in Galicia. His battlefield successes and his close political affiliation with Pilsudski ensured him a prominent place in the postwar army. Pilsudski selected him as his successor largely due to his apparent lack of interest in politics. Unfortunately, his ambitions were whetted and he began to cast himself as a supreme leader in both political and military matters. Given the enormity of Poland's predicament, Rydz-Smigly floundered in both the political and military realms.

Poland had a number of capable generals in 1939, but the politicisation of the army in the 1930s and the cult of amateurism and improvisation inherited from Pilsudski led to a weak system of command and control. While the German forces participating in the campaign had army groups to control the field armies, in the Polish case the nine major field-army commanders reported back directly to Rydz-Smigly. Given the relatively poor communication links between Warsaw and the field armies, this ensured delays in decision-making, and the Polish command system could not cope.

RED ARMY COMMANDERS

The Red Army was still in a state of shock from Stalin's purges when it was thrust into Poland in September 1939. Having liquidated much of the senior army leadership in 1937–38, Stalin was at a loss to fill key positions. Several of the survivors, including **Georgi Zhukov**, were in the Far East at the time, engaged in combat with the Japanese at Khalkin Gol. One of the last surviving members of Stalin's military circle from the Civil War days, **Semyon Timoshenko**, was appointed to command the main element of the strike force, the Ukrainian front. The Byelorussian front was led by an inexperienced and lacklustre corps commander, **M.P. Kovalev**. The same situation was repeated through the lower levels of the force with divisional commanders assigned to corps, battalion commanders to regiments and so on. The only advantage that the Polish campaign offered to the Red Army was to help identify the more skilled young commanders who had so precipitously risen through the ranks due to the purges. Vasily Chuikov, later a hero of Stalingrad, was among these rising stars of the Red Army.

OPPOSING PLANS

Early German studies of military actions against Poland included both a small campaign to seize the Pomeranian corridor and Danzig, and a full-scale campaign. World reaction to the absorption of the Czech lands in March 1939 and the ensuing partial Polish mobilisation rendered a surprise seizure of Danzig unlikely. As a result, Hitler ordered the OKH to begin planning a full-scale invasion in detail, codenamed Case White (*Fall Weiss*). Poland's precarious geography simplified the process. With Slovakia a German puppet, German armed forces could attack Poland from three sides. Furthermore, Poland had few natural defences. The country's name stems from the Slavic word for fields, and most of the western portion of the country was flat farmland. The only natural obstruction was the Carpathian mountain chain between Poland and Slovakia, but this was not intended as a major theatre of operations.

Due to concern over the possible reaction of the Western powers, the primary aim of the German planners was to ensure an extremely rapid destruction of the Polish army so that forces could be shifted westward to defend against French action. As a result, the objective became the envelopment and destruction of the Polish army west of the Vistula and Narew rivers, in a classic Prussian encirclement. A twin-pincer movement from Prussia and Silesia was intended to envelope the bulk of Polish forces in western Poland. The heaviest concentration of forces was with Rundstedt's Army Group South. The main blow would be struck from Silesia towards the north-east, aimed at Warsaw. Rundstedt's main concern was the Eighth Army, which would cover the northern flank against Polish forces in Pomerania. This army was relatively weak, many of the divisions were new, and some had no march or combat training. A secondary blow would be directed out of the former Czech territories and Slovakia to deal with Polish forces in Galicia.

The task of Army Group North was more challenging because of the geography. The initial mission of Bock's forces would be to push across the Pomeranian corridor to link East Prussia with the rest of Germany. Once forces were in place, Army Group North would push southward towards Warsaw. Bock's task was complicated by the terrain along the Prussian frontier, which was more wooded and cluttered by water obstacles than Rundstedt's Silesian thrust. The initial planning aimed at a direct assault on Warsaw from the north, along the western bank of the Vistula. Bock wanted more freedom of action so that his forces could travel down the east side of the Vistula to cut off any Polish forces that might attempt to escape. His request was initially denied, as the OKW did not want major forces to become entangled in the east in case they had to be shifted back to the front with France.

Mobilisation and deployment of the Wehrmacht had to be concealed so as not to compromise German diplomatic efforts in late August, which were aimed at isolating Poland. The first stage of the deployment began on 26 June with the transfer of nine infantry divisions to the east. The second phase, involving 13 divisions, began on 3 August and was disguised as normal summer manoeuvres. The deployment, which involved the first major transport of units into East Prussia, was disguised as a manoeuvre by the East Prussian 1st Army Corps and the annual Tannenberg celebration, which in 1939 happened to be the 25th anniversary of the First World War victory. The next wave of mobilisation began on 19 August and involved all those formations that were six days or more away from their assembly areas on the Polish frontier. Since the original plan called for the start of the operation on 26 August, all the major formations were in place by 25 August.

German intelligence on Polish dispositions was poor; this was in part due to German weaknesses in intelligence gathering, but also due to the conviction that the Polish army could be readily defeated. These intelligence shortcomings had little consequence in 1939, but would become more manifest in 1941 following the invasion of the Soviet Union.

Halder and Brauchitsch discuss the Case White plan. The plan reflected the traditional Prussian style of grand envelopment. (NARA)

In early 1939, the Polish general staff began to re-examine its 1936 studies about a potential war with Germany in light of new intelligence information about its powerful neighbour. Like many small nations, Poland devoted a great deal of effort to intelligence gathering and had both an effective human-intelligence and signals-intelligence network. The Poles had broken the German Enigma tactical coding system, though the German addition of another element to the system in the summer of 1939 cut off this means of intelligence gathering. Nevertheless, the Poles had a good appreciation of German tactical dispositions and a clear understanding of the likely German plan. A new war plan, codenamed Plan Z (*Zachod* – West) was submitted in early March 1939. The plan estimated that Germany could mobilise about 110 division-sized formations, of which about 70 would be committed initially against Poland before being shifted to the west. Plan Z had to be reformulated after the seizure of the Czech lands on 15 March. The earlier 1936 war plan and the first draft of Plan Z assumed that the main German thrust would come from Pomerania striking to the south-east.

The revised plan correctly recognised that the main effort would now more likely be from Silesia striking to the north-east. In May 1939, discussions were held with the French general staff to discuss joint actions in the event of a German attack. Although the Poles left France convinced that the French army would launch a major attack against Germany involving between 35 and 38 divisions within two weeks of an attack on Poland, in fact Gamelin and the French general staff had no detailed plan for such an operation. Indeed, on 31 May 1939, a general directive changed the scope of the offensive to a 'feeling out operation', but the Poles were never informed of this change. The French expected that the Poles could hold out for three or four months, more than enough time for a proper operation to be prepared. The illusory Polish

The French chief of staff, General Maurice Gamelin, observes Polish wargames during a visit in the 1930s. The Polish minister for military affairs, General Tadeusz Kasprzycki is on Gamelin's left. In spite of their important military ties, France had little influence on Polish war planning. (J. Janik)

conviction that there would be an immediate French attack in the west lay at the heart of the Poles' strategic planning in 1939.

The Poles examined two broad strategic options for defence. The first, promoted by the French army's General Maxime Weygand, was to rely on the old Russian fortification line along the Biebrza, Narew, Vistula, and San river lines. This line fitted Polish operational doctrine, since such a defensive grouping would not overextend the limited Polish force structure of 30 divisions. Its main problem was political. For such a plan to succeed, the Polish army would have to be fully mobilised and deployed, since the majority of Polish troops had to be called up from the more populous provinces west of this defensive line. It was the presumption of Plan Z that Germany would strike before mobilisation could be fully implemented; this being the case, much of the manpower of the army would be lost before they could reach their mobilisation areas east of the river line. The other important factor that undermined support for this option was the recent examples of German military and diplomatic action. There was considerable concern that if Poland's defences were situated so far eastward, the Germans would simply seize the Pomeranian corridor as well as the western provinces of Pomerania and Silesia unopposed, just as they had taken the Sudetenland. If Germany did so, it would create the impression that Poland was unwilling to fight in its own defence, thereby undermining British and French commitments to take joint military action against Germany. The Polish government was unequivocally opposed to any plan that could lead to a repeat of Czechoslovakia's uncontested demise.

The second plan was to position Polish troops well forward of the river line near the western frontier. It was presumed that it would take 12 to 15 days to fully mobilise the army, so the defence of the western borders in the initial phase of the operation would serve to shield the mobilisation of forces in the most populous sections of western Poland. This was especially critical as Poland was an ethnically diverse country and only about 60 per cent of the population was Polish. The Polish population was most heavily concentrated in the west, while the eastern provinces were heavily Byelorussian and Ukrainian. Since the army relied more on recruits drawn from the Polish provinces, this was a vital concern.

In addition, a strong defence of the western region would oblige Britain and France to honour their commitments to declare war on Germany. The Polish planners were under no illusions about the prospects for the small Polish army against the much larger and better equipped German army. The Poles' only hope was to prolong the defence long enough for France and Britain to mobilise and strike Germany in the west.

The resulting plan placed the bulk of Polish forces in western Poland. It is a tactic that has been widely misinterpreted in many histories of the war as a plan for a linear, static defence of the frontier on the model of the French plans. However, it had little to do with French doctrine since there were minimal border fortifications. Instead, the objective was to shield the western Polish provinces for as long as possible to enable mobilisation, and to permit a gradual withdrawal of forces eastward to prolong the war by avoiding decisive battle. Polish defensive concepts were based largely on the experience of the 1920 war with Russia, which had been a war of manoeuvre. Rydz-Smigly's intention was to withdraw the army eastward and to avoid decisive battle west of the Vistula.

There were several major flaws in the plan. The disposition of the forces forced the infantry divisions to cover sectors far beyond that deemed prudent in Polish tactical doctrine. As a result, the forward divisions were never able to effectively slow the German advance without becoming deeply engaged and destroyed by the larger and more powerful German forces. In addition, the plan seriously underestimated the pace of fighting. Although the Poles planned to wage a war of manoeuvre, they failed to appreciate the impact that mechanisation had had upon the Wehrmacht. The low density of understrength Polish divisions ensured the penetration of the main line of resistance by fully mobilised German formations, and once a penetration occurred, the Wehrmacht had the capability to exploit their achievements much more quickly than the Poles could react.

The Poles were not the only nation to underestimate the potential of the new style of mechanised warfare and, since the Polish campaign was its first demonstration, the Polish attitude was unsurprising. Like most other European armies, they had been misled by the lessons of the recent Spanish Civil War, in which tanks and aircraft had been used in significant numbers without affecting the pace of modern combat.

The Polish predicament was that the river defence option, while militarily sound, failed to address Poland's political and strategic dilemmas. The forward defence plan, while addressing Poland's political and strategic concerns, was militarily unsound. Poland was in a hopeless situation when facing its more powerful western neighbour. The situation became even more grim in late August with the announcement of the Molotov–Ribbentrop agreement. The Polish government was unaware of the secret invasion protocols of the non-aggression pact, and so it was unclear whether the Soviet Union would take military action in the event of a war between Poland and Germany. Given the paucity of forces available to the Polish army, there was no shift in dispositions as a result of the pact and the eastern borders remained unprotected except for token border forces.

OPPOSING ARMIES

The Wehrmacht enjoyed numerous advantages over the Polish army in both quality and quantity. German superiority was in no small measure due to the enormous economic disparity between the two countries. Although Poland devoted a significant share of its gross national product to the armed forces, its defence expenditure was dwarfed by Germany's. In the period 1935–39, Germany had defence budgets totalling about $24 billion; 30 times greater than Poland's expenditure of $760 million during the same period. The differences were most noticeable in the technical branches of the service, such as the air force and navy.

In terms of peacetime strength, the German army was more than three times the size of the Polish; about 600,000 men compared to about 210,000. The mobilisation potential of Germany was also considerably greater, with an active force of 51 divisions and a wartime force of 102 divisions. Poland was able to muster only 30 divisions, though theoretically another 15 reserve divisions could eventually be deployed in a protracted conflict.

The Wehrmacht committed its best divisions to the Polish campaign and left units with less training and equipment facing the French. In total, the two army groups deployed 37 infantry divisions, one mountain division, four motorised infantry divisions, four light divisions, six Panzer divisions, a cavalry brigade and a variety of border units, gendarme and other paramilitary formations. For the invasion of Poland, Army Group North had a total of 630,000 personnel earmarked, with a further 886,000 allocated to the more powerful Army Group South.

Germany embraced army motorisation as part of its defence reforms of the early 1930s. Here, a German motor column passes through a Polish village in 1939 on Krupp Protze light trucks. (NARA)

The extent of German motorisation has often been exaggerated. Horses were still the primary means of transportation for most infantry divisions, like this team pulling a 75mm infantry gun. (NARA)

As of 1 September, the Polish army had deployed 23 regular infantry divisions, three reserve infantry divisions, eight cavalry brigades, three mountain brigades, and one motorised brigade as well as some border troops and other paramilitary formations. In terms of combat power, the Wehrmacht fielded the equivalent of 559 infantry battalions against 376 on the Polish side. This was a force ratio of 1.5:1 in the German favour overall, though if assessing the force ratios only along the major avenues of attack, the Wehrmacht enjoyed a 2.3:1 force advantage. In field artillery, the Wehrmacht deployed 5,805 guns compared with Poland's 2,065 for a force advantage of 2.8:1 overall and 4.4:1 along the main avenues of attack. The force disparities were greatest in armoured forces, with the Wehrmacht deploying 2,511 tanks to Poland's 615, for an advantage of 4.1:1 overall and 8.2:1 along the main avenues of attack. These numerical comparisons underestimate the German strength advantages, since many Polish formations were only partially mobilised while German units were on war footing at the outset of the campaign.

The most obvious qualitative disparity between the two forces was in the greater mechanisation of the Wehrmacht. Germany had formed six Panzer divisions and four light divisions starting in 1935, while Poland fielded only a single mechanised brigade. The German army in the First World War had been slow to adopt tanks, but the role of Allied tank formations in the 1918 defeat convinced many German officers of the need to embrace this new technology. During Seeckt's reforms of the Reichswehr in the 1920s, extensive experimentation was carried out with mechanised formations, even though Germany was not allowed tanks under the terms of the Versailles treaty. The project was continued by Seeckt's successors, and during the 1932

The most overlooked innovation in the German reforms of the 1930s was the widespread application of radio to command and control. Radio enabled Panzer units to co-ordinate their actions with neighbouring units and their supporting arms, making combined arms warfare possible. This is a Befehlspanzer III, based on the PzKpfw. III medium tank. (NARA)

ABOVE **The German tank force was still heavily dependent on light, machine-gun armed tanks like this PzKpfw I, seen here on a smoke-filled street in Warsaw in late September 1939. It was the most common tank in German use in 1939, with some 1,445 in service. The PzKpfw I proved to be a disappointment in combat and they were withdrawn from service as quickly as possible. (NARA)**

ABOVE, RIGHT **Armoured cars were an inexpensive alternative to tanks for reconnaissance operations and were used in large numbers in 1939 with over 1,000 in service. However, their mobility was restricted by the poor road conditions in the east and tracked vehicles increasingly took their place as the war dragged on. This is an SdKfz 222 armed with a 20mm automatic cannon, followed by a machine-gun armed SdKfz 221. These vehicles were used in the reconnaissance battalion of light, motorised infantry and Panzer divisions. (NARA)**

manoeuvres, a motorised cavalry corps was deployed. Even the infantry experimented with motorised reconnaissance. When German remilitarisation began in 1933 under Hitler, the groundwork had already been established for further mechanisation.

In contrast to many other armies, the Wehrmacht committed none of its tank strength to separate battalions for close infantry support. Instead, armoured advocates like Heinz Guderian insisted that the Panzers should be concentrated into divisions with their own combat mission. Guderian argued that these formations had the power to overcome enemy infantry defences on their own by shock and firepower. Once the enemy's main line of resistance had been penetrated, their mobility would allow them to rapidly exploit the penetration by either enveloping the enemy from the rear in a pincer movement with neighbouring Panzer units, or racing deep into enemy territory to attack key command and supply nodes. These views were criticised by some older German generals, but they won the personal approval of Adolf Hitler. The Panzer divisions were part of a broader effort to adopt combined arms tactics and they were actually mixed formations of tanks, motorised infantry and motorised artillery. The power of a Panzer division came from its ability to exploit the virtues of all three arms of service to accomplish the mission. One of the Panzer division's least appreciated advantages was its extensive deployment of radios. Guderian was a signals officer and realised the need for radios to co-ordinate fast-moving mobile formations. The radios were a critical ingredient in combined arms operations, since they gave the various formations the ability to communicate with each other and synchronise their actions. No other European army had so successfully integrated radio into their command and control structure. The French army, for example, had a very poor distribution of radios to mechanised

formations. The Germans deployed radios in a large percentage of their tanks, and unit commanders travelled in a type of radio-equipped tank called a *befehlspanzer*. Most of the 215 *befehlspanzer* in service in 1939 were a turretless type based on the PzKpfw I chassis, but 38 were the more capable PzBefWg III on the medium-tank chassis.

The light divisions, which were an attempt to mechanise the German cavalry, were more controversial than the Panzer divisions as some generals, including Rundstedt, felt that horse cavalry divisions would still be needed if operating in eastern Europe due to the poor roads. Hitler had an aversion to horses and settled the matter in favour of the French model of dragoons with a small armoured element. The resulting divisions were intended to function in the traditional cavalry role of strategic reconnaissance and flank security. Compared with the

A German infantry company on the march into Poland in September 1939. Like most armies of the time, the German infantry was dependent on horses and bicycles for mobility even though it had more motor vehicles than its Polish opponents. (NARA)

One of the signature weapons of the German infantry in the Second World War was the MG34 machine gun, seen here in action in Poland in 1939. It was lightweight and had a very high rate of fire, necessitating frequent barrel changes. The soldier to the left is carrying a spare barrel in the container on his back. (NARA)

Panzer divisions, they had fewer tanks and more motorised infantry.

German tanks in 1939 were not particularly impressive in terms of either firepower or armour compared with models used later in the war. The majority were light tanks including the machine-gun armed PzKpfw I and the slightly larger PzKpfw II, which made up three-quarters of the force. While the PzKpfw I is sometimes dismissed as a training tank, this was certainly not the case. Like most armies of the 1930s, the Germans felt that a machine-gun armament would be adequate for most missions. Tank-versus-tank fighting was almost unheard of until the Second World War. Previously, the main mission of tanks was seen as defeating enemy infantry. The fighting during the Spanish Civil War (1936–39) made it

Radios proved important not only to the mobile forces but also to the infantry. This German infantry radio team is seen in operation during the fighting near Warsaw in September 1939. They are operating a Tornister Funkgerat d2 transmitter-receiver. Each infantry division had a radio company, divided into 21 radio sections, four with this particular type of set. (NARA)

clear that more attention had to be paid to the enemy tank threat. In Spain, the Condor Legion's PzKpfw Is stood little chance against Soviet T-26 tanks armed with 45mm guns, and the Nationalists preferred to use captured T-26s rather than the weakly armed German tanks. There were 1,445 PzKpfw I in service in September 1939. The PzKpfw II was a better design, and its 20mm gun could penetrate the armour of any Polish tank of the period. Nevertheless, such a weapon was of little use in suppressing enemy anti-tank guns or troops in field fortifications. PzKpfw IIs were almost as numerous as the PzKpfw I, with 1,223 in service in September 1939.

The light tanks were supported by small numbers of medium tanks. The PzKpfw III was a new medium tank armed with a 37mm gun. While it would become the mainstay of the Panzer force in the years of victory in 1940–42, there were only 98 in service in 1939, with a dozen in each Panzer division. The larger PzKpfw IV was intended to provide fire support for the light tanks and was armed with a short-barrelled 75mm gun; there were 211 in service in 1939, normally six per regiment. In total, these medium types made up only about ten per cent of the Panzer force in 1939. Germany also benefited from the absorption of the Czech tank force, which was used in two of the light divisions. A total of 196 PzKpfw 35(t) and 78 PzKpfw 38(t) were in service in 1939, representing about eight per cent of the Panzer force. Of the 3,466 tanks available on 1 September 1939, 2,626 were committed to the Polish campaign. Germany also had a significant force of armoured cars, including 718 light armoured cars such as the SdKfz 221, 222 and 223, and 307 heavy armoured cars such as the SdKfz 231 and 232. Armoured cars were used in the reconnaissance regiments of the light, motorised infantry, and Panzer divisions.

Poland's armoured force was weak compared to Germany's though not as back-

The Polish infantry was well equipped with modern small arms, relying on a locally manufactured version of the German Mauser 98k as its standard rifle. The field uniform was similar to that worn by their German counterparts, but in a khaki colour. The Polish army adopted a new steel helmet in 1936, reminiscent of the later US army helmet in shape. (Pilsudksi Institute)

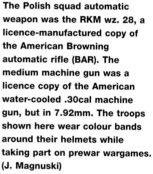

The Polish squad automatic weapon was the RKM wz. 28, a licence-manufactured copy of the American Browning automatic rifle (BAR). The medium machine gun was a licence copy of the American water-cooled .30cal machine gun, but in 7.92mm. The troops shown here wear colour bands around their helmets while taking part on prewar wargames. (J. Magnuski)

ward as is so often assumed. Like the Italians, the Poles had been bitten by the tankette fever of the early 1930s and they had based their armoured force on hundreds of small, machine-gun armed TK and TKS tankettes. Neither vehicle had anti-armour capability and their speed and mobility were poor. They were not really suitable for anything other than direct support, and their premature acquisition served as a dead-weight on further Polish mechanisation. At the beginning of the September campaign, the Polish army deployed about 450 TK and TKS tankettes in 13 squadrons attached to the cavalry, 17 companies attached to the infantry, and ten platoons attached to armoured trains.

Poland soon recognised the limits of tankettes and turned to Britain with a small order for Vickers 6-ton tanks. A total of 38 were purchased, 16 with 47mm guns and 22 of a twin-turret design with a machine gun in each turret. During the September campaign, these tanks served in the two mechanised brigades. Under the 1936 rearmament programme, Poland began producing an improved version of the Vickers under

Polish field artillery was not particularly modern. This wz. 02/26 75mm gun is a rechambered version of the Tsarist 3in. Model 02. A total of 466 of these guns were in service in 1939. Each cavalry brigade had a horse artillery battery with 12–16 of these guns. (Pilsudski Institute)

licence. The resultant tank, which had a new diesel engine, was the 7TP light tank. The first 40 were completed with twin machine-gun turrets, and the final 95 finished before the war had a new single turret armed with a Bofors 37mm gun. The single-turret 7TP was better than most German tanks in 1939 but there were too few to make much difference. The Poles equipped two battalions, with a third battalion being formed, and these battalions were independent formations attached at army level for armoured support. Poland attempted to make up the shortfall by acquiring French Somua and British Matilda tanks in 1939, but only received a single battalion of French Renault R-35 infantry tanks just weeks before the start of the campaign. This battalion was only partially mobilised in 1939 and saw little fighting. Poland also fielded ten armoured trains; a legacy of the 1920 war experience. Armoured trains had proved a vital source of mobile artillery firepower in the war with the Bolsheviks, but, like Zeppelins, they were a technology whose time had passed. Despite proving their worth in the 1939 fighting, armoured trains were much too vulnerable to air attack, with four of the ten being lost in this fashion.

In contrast to Germany, Poland still maintained large cavalry formations in 1939. The cavalry divisions had been abolished but the remaining eight cavalry brigades were still considered the elite of the

Although most Polish weapons were foreign types manufactured under licence, there were some local designs. Three wz. 36 46mm infantry mortars were deployed in each infantry company. The example on the left without the baseplate is the standard wz. 36, while the example to the right is the original version tested in 1932–33. (Ordnance Museum, APG)

The Polish wz. 35 anti-tank rifle was the infantry's primary means of anti-tank defence with 92 per division. Although it was similar to German anti-tank rifles used in the First World War, it pioneered the use of tungsten-cored projectiles, which enabled it to penetrate the armour of nearly any of the German tanks in service in 1939. Unfortunately, the ammunition was so secret that the rifles were not distributed until the September mobilisation, limiting their use. (Author)

army. The retention of the horse cavalry was in no small measure due to the importance and success of the horse cavalry in the 1920 war with the Bolsheviks, and the continued orientation of the Polish war plans towards defence against the Soviet Union. Horse cavalry was essential in the borderlands with the Soviet Union, which lacked a decent road network and contained the vast Pripyat marshlands. As the threat from Germany grew in the mid-1930s, the army began to debate the need to mechanise the cavalry. While traditionalists were an impediment to mechanisation, the real problem was the puny Polish defence budget. Two cavalry brigades were mechanised, though only one was fully ready on 1 September 1939. Contrary to the popular myth, the lance had been dropped as a weapon in the mid-1930s and the Polish cavalry fought like most other European cavalry of the time. The horse provided mobility and the cavalry generally fought dismounted with rifles and other infantry weapons. The sabre was retained for when opportunities presented themselves for a mounted attack. The Polish cavalry's main advantage was the quality of troops and the regiments continued to attract some of the best officers and men. The cavalry brigades contained a squadron with tankettes and armoured cars, but these vehicles were not popular due to their poor off-road mobility and unreliability. The miserable qualities of these outdated armoured vehicles helped poison the Polish view of the potential of mechanised tactics.

Of all the combat arms, the German and Polish infantry divisions were most closely matched in terms of organisation and equipment. Both forces were based around three infantry regiments with a total personnel strength of about 16,500. Both sides employed Mauser 98k as their principal rifle, though some Polish reserve formations had other weapons. The German squads were beginning to receive the MP38 submachine guns in small numbers by 1939, while the Poles had a handful of the new Mors submachine guns in service in 1939. The German army was beginning to adopt the MG34 light machine gun in significant numbers, while the Polish army employed a licence copy of the American Browning Automatic Rifle (BAR) as its principal squad automatic weapon. The German divisions had more firepower at most organisational levels, with a total of 735 light machine guns versus 326 in Polish units.

Anti-tank defence in both armies was similar. The German army used the 37mm PaK 36 anti-tank gun, while Polish infantry used the licence-manufactured Swedish Bofors 37mm anti-tank gun. Both had similar

performance and could penetrate any tank of the period. In the Polish case, they were deployed in platoons at battalion level for a total of 27 per division. In the German case, they were deployed in companies at regimental level with 12 guns each. The German infantry divisions had slightly more anti-tank guns than comparable Polish divisions, as they also had a separate anti-tank unit at divisional level in addition to the three companies at regimental level. Both the German and Polish armies deployed anti-tank rifles for company defence. The German army used the Panzerbusche 38/39, while the Poles used the wz. 35 anti-tank rifle. The two weapons had similar performance; each was able to penetrate about 30mm (1.1in) of armour at 100m (110yds), which was more than adequate against the poorly armoured tanks of the period.

The firepower disparity was greatest in artillery. Even though the total number of tubes was only slightly greater in the German case (68 versus 48), the actual salvo power was about double that of the Polish divisional artillery. The Wehrmacht relied on the 105mm leFH 18 as its principal field gun, which was a more modern and powerful weapon than the Polish 75mm field guns based on the French M.1897 and rechambered Russian Mod. 02/26. For heavy firepower, the Germans relied on the modern sFH 18 while the Poles used a mixed bag of Skoda Mod. 14/19 100mm howitzers, 105mm Mod. 29 Schneider guns and 155mm Schneider Mod. 17 howitzers. In addition, German infantry divisions had 20 75mm and 150mm infantry guns for direct support, for which the Poles had no equivalents. The German firepower advantage was not only in the number and calibre of tubes, but also in ammunition supply and fire control. Due to greater use of radios, German artillery fire control was a generation beyond that of the Poles who still relied on First World War techniques. In addition, the greater motorisation of the German forces meant that the Wehrmacht divisions

The mechanisation of two Polish cavalry brigades led to some modernisation of the field artillery. The standard French Mle. 97 75mm gun was made suitable for motorised traction by the addition of a new suspension and pneumatic tyres. This particular battery served with the 10th Mechanised Brigade. (J. Magnuski)

Armoured support for infantry and cavalry units was provided by the small TK and TKS tankettes. There was a company of 13 in each infantry division and a squadron of 13 in each cavalry brigade. Here, they are seen on prewar manoeuvres with an infantry company. (J. Magnuski)

had more ammunition on hand, and could replenish the gun batteries in a more timely fashion. A German division carried with it some 230 tonnes of artillery ammunition, an impossible amount for the Poles due to a lack of trucks. Although much has been made of the damage caused by Stuka attacks, it was in fact the German artillery that had the most devastating effect on the Polish infantry during the fighting. The effect was even greater at corps and army level, with the Wehrmacht having advantages in both the number and quality of heavy-calibre weapons.

Although both sides relied on horses as their principal means of transport and supply, the Wehrmacht infantry divisions were more heavily motorised than the Polish units. The Wehrmacht infantry division had 5,375 horses, 938 motor vehicles and 530 motorcycles compared with 6,937 horses and only 76 motor vehicles per Polish division. The difference reflected the greater wealth of the German economy, which before the war had about 1.4 million motor vehicles compared with only about 33,000 in Poland. In terms of command and control, the German divisions had a motorised radio company in addition to a field-telephone company while the Poles relied almost exclusively on field telephones. In a war of manoeuvre, the new means of communication were a vital ingredient in German victory; they not only enhanced the tactical advantages of the Wehrmacht in areas such as artillery firepower, but also made it possible to exploit aerial reconnaissance to rapidly manoeuvre German formations and to synchronise the activities of neighbouring German units faster than the Poles could react.

The Germans enjoyed a substantial advantage in air power. Total German aircraft strength on 1 September 1939 was 3,368 combat aircraft, of which about 64 per cent was committed to the Polish

campaign. The main striking force was divided into two formations: Luftflotte 1 (supporting Bock's Army Group North); and Luftflotte 4 (supporting Rundstedt's Army Group South). These units included 800 medium bombers, 340 Stuka dive-bombers, 520 fighters and 250 transport aircraft. In addition, there were organic aviation-support units directly attached to each army for spotting and liaison work, totalling 94 aircraft in Army Group North and 168 in Army Group South. Front-line German aviation strength against Poland in 1939 was 2,152 aircraft. The German bomber force was made up primarily of the Heinkel He-111 and Dornier Do-17, with a handful of Ju-88 beginning to enter service. The fighter force was made up of a combination of 440 single-engine Messerschmidt Bf-109 and about 80 twin-engine Bf-110 aircraft. Army-support aircraft included the Henschel Hs-126 observation aircraft and some older scout types like the He-46. The army-support units also had their own organic reconnaissance unit, usually a squadron with Dornier Do-17P aircraft. During the Polish campaign, the Luftwaffe committed all of its Stuka force, about 70 per cent of its bombers and 50 per cent of its fighters.

Although the Polish air force had a nominal strength of 1,900 aircraft, 650 of these planes were trainers and another 700 were obsolete types and in many cases not functional. The real strength was 392 front-line combat aircraft including 158 fighters, 114 scout bombers, 36 medium bombers and 84 observation aircraft. There were also about 100 support aircraft including the RWD 8 light aircraft and the old Fokker F.VII transport. The Polish fighter force was made up of 128 PZL P.11 and 30 older PZL P.7 fighters. Both types were high-wing monoplane fighters with open cockpits and fixed undercarriages. They were excellent fighters when first put into service in the early 1930s, but were a generation behind the German Bf-109. Their intended

Poland purchased 39 Vickers 6-ton light tanks in 1931 including 16 of this model with the 47mm gun. An improved type was licence produced in Poland as the 7TP light tank. The original Vickers, after some local modifications, were assigned to the two mechanised cavalry brigades. (J. Magnuski)

replacement, the PZL P.50 *Jastrzeb*, was still in development when war broke out. The PZL P.23 *Karas* was an army co-operation aircraft patterned after the aircraft that had served so well in the 1920 war. The *Karas* was intended for reconnaissance and light bombing and was a cross between the German Hs-126 and Ju-87 Stuka. The best and most modern Polish warplane was the PZL P.37 *Los* medium bomber but they were only beginning to enter service when war broke out. Some thought had been given to employing *Los* bombers in attacks on targets inside Germany, but in the event, their main mission was the interdiction of enemy supply columns. Observation aircraft included 35 RWD 14 *Czapla* and 49 of the older R-XIII. Reserves included 47 incomplete *Los* bombers, 50 P.11 and 30 P.7 fighters, and about 60 P.23 *Karas*. The air force was divided into two main components – strategic aviation and army aviation. The strategic aviation force (*Lotnictwo Dyspozycyne*) consisted of the Bomber Brigade with 36 P.37 *Los* and 50 P.23 *Karas*. It also included the Pursuit Brigade for the defence of Warsaw with 43 P.11 and ten P.7 fighters. The army aviation (*Lotnictwo Armijne*) typically deployed a scout squadron with P.23 *Karas*, one or more fighter squadrons with P.11, an observation squadron with RWD 14 *Czapla*, and a communication unit with RWD 8 light aircraft with each army. The exact number of squadrons with each army varied. In total, the strategic aviation units contained 146 combat aircraft and 60 assorted support and transport aircraft, while the army aviation had 246 combat aircraft and 42 support aircraft.

France and Britain agreed to reinforce Poland with more modern aircraft to make up for the deficiencies in its aviation units. France was on the verge of delivering Morane Saulnier Ms.406 fighters, while Britain was preparing Hurricane fighters and Fairey Battle light bombers, but none of these aircraft arrived before the start of the campaign.

The navies on both sides played a minor role in the conflict. The Polish navy was configured primarily for operations against possible Soviet operations in the Baltic. Its main ports were so near Germany that in the event of war, they could be quickly smothered from the air. The main element was the destroyer flotilla, consisting of two French *Simoun*-class destroyers, ORP *Wicher* and *Burza* delivered in 1932, and two Polish-designed destroyers built in Britain in 1937, the *Grom* and *Blyskawica*. The submarine flotilla included three mine-laying submarines, ORP *Rys*, *Wilk* and *Zbik*, delivered from France between 1931 and 1932, and two ocean-going submarines, *Orzel* and *Sep*, delivered by the Netherlands in 1939. The only other major surface combatant was the ORP *Gryf* minelayer. There were a number of smaller auxiliaries and the navy also had a small air arm and coastal defence batteries.

The German Kriegsmarine, aware of the Polish mine-laying capability and submarine force, decided to limit its operations in the Baltic and leave it up to the Luftwaffe to deal with the threat. When word was received that the Polish destroyer flotilla had departed for Britain on 31 August, the cruisers and some of the destroyers originally earmarked for Naval Command East were transferred to Naval Command West. During the Polish campaign, Naval Group East deployed four older warships including the cadet-training battleship *Schleswig-Holstein*, 14 submarines, nine destroyers, 34 torpedo boats and other small combatants, 26 minesweepers and three aviation units.

POLISH ARMY ORDER OF BATTLE, 1 SEPTEMBER 1939

Army Pomorze	**GenDiv W. Bortnowski**
9th Infantry Division	Col J. Werobej
15th Infantry Division	BrigGen Z. Przyjalkowski
27th Infantry Division	BrigGen J. Drapella
Group Wschod	**BrigGen M. Boltuc**
4th Infantry Division	Col T. L. Lubicz-Niezabitowski
16th Infantry Division	Col S. Switalski
Group Czersk	**BrigGen Grzmot-Skotnicki**
Pomorska Cavalry Brigade	Col A. Zakrzewski

Army Modlin	**BrigGen E. Krukowicz-Przedrzymirski**
8th Infantry Division	Col T.W. Furgalski
20th Infantry Division	Col W.A. Lawin-Liszka
Nowogrodzka Cavalry Brigade	BrigGen W. Anders
Mazowiecka Cavalry Brigade	Col Jan Karcz

Operational Group Wyszkow	**BrigGen W. Kowalski**
1st Legion Infantry Division	BrigGen W. Kowalski
41st Reserve Infantry Division	BrigGen W. Piekarski

Special Operational Group Narew	**BrigGen C. Mlot-Fijalkowski**
18th Infantry Division	Col S. Kossecki
33rd Reserve Infantry Division	Col T. Kalina-Zieleniewski
Podlaska Cavalry Brigade	BrigGen L. Kmicic-Skrzynski
Suwalska Cavalry Brigade	BrigGen Z. Podhorski

Army Poznan	**GenDiv T. Kutrzeba**
14th Infantry Division	BrigGen F. Wlad
17th Wielkopolska Infantry Division	Col M.S. Mozdyniewicz
25th Infantry Division	BrigGen F. Alter
26th Infantry Division	Col A. Brzechwa-Ajdukiewicz
Wielkopolska Cavalry Brigade	BrigGen R. Abraham
Podolska Cavalry Brigade	Col L. Strzelecki

Army Lodz	**GenDiv J.K. Rommel**
2nd Legion Infantry Division	Col E. Dojan-Surowka
10th Infantry Division	BrigGen F. Dindorf-Ankowicz
28th Infantry Division	BrigGen Boncza-Uzdowski
Kresowa Cavalry Brigade	Col S. Kulesza
Group Piotrkow	**BrigGen W. Thommee**
30th Infantry Division	BrigGen L.O. Cehak
Wolynska Cavalry Brigade	Col J. Filipowicz

Army Prusy	**GenDiv S. Dab-Biernacki**
13th Infantry Division	Col W. Zuborz-Kalinski
29th Infantry Division	Col I.J. Ozierewicz
Cavalry Operational Group	**BrigGen R. Dreszer**
19th Infantry Division	BrigGen K. Kwaciszewski
Wilenska Cavalry Brigade	Col K. Drucki-Lubecki
Skwarczynski Operational Group	**BrigGen Skwarczynski**
3rd Legion Infantry Division	Col M. Turkowski
12th Infantry Division	BrigGen G. Paszkiewicz
36th Reserve Infantry Division	Col B.A. Ostrowski

Army Krakow	**BrigGen A. Szylling**
6th Infantry Division	BrigGen B.S. Mond
7th Infantry Division	BrigGen I.T. Gasiorowski
10th Mechanised Brigade	Col S. Maczek
Krakowska Cavalry Brigade	BrigGen Z. Piasecki
Group Slask	**BrigGen J. Jagmin-Sadowski**
23rd Gornoslaska Infantry Division	Col W. P. Powierza
55th Reserve Infantry Division	Col S. Kolabinski
Group Bielsko	**BrigGen M. Boruta-Spiechowicz**
1st Mountain Brigade	Col E. Zondolowicz
21st Mountain Infantry Division	BrigGen J. Kustron

Army Karpaty	**GenDiv K. Fabrycy**
2nd Mountain Brigade	Col A. Stawarz
3rd Mountain Brigade	Col J. Kotowicz

GERMAN ARMY ORDER OF BATTLE, 1 SEPTEMBER 1939

Army Group North	**ColGen Fedor Von Bock**
73rd Infantry Division	MajGen F. von Rabenau
10th Light Division	MajGen Schaal
206th Infantry Division	LtGen H. Hoefl
208th Infantry Division	LtGen M. Andreas

Fourth Army	**Gen der Artillerie Gunther Von Kluge**
218th Infantry Division	MajGen W. Fhr. Grote
Frontier Guard Command	*Gen Der Flieger Leonhard Kaupisch*
207th Infantry Division	MajGen K. von Tiedemann
19th Corps	*Gen der Panzertruppe Heinz Guderian*
2nd Motorised Division	LtGen P. Bader
3rd Panzer Division	LtGen L. Frh. Geyr von Schweppenburg
20th Motorised Division	LtGen M. von Wiktorin
2nd Corps	*Gen der Infanterie Erich Straub*
32nd Infantry Division	LtGen F. Boehme
3rd Infantry Division	MajGen W. Lichel
3rd Corps	*Gen der Artillerie Curt Haase*
Netze Division	MajGen Frh. von Gablenz
50th Infantry Division	LtGen K. Sorsche

Third Army	**Gen der Artillerie Georg Von Kuchler**
217th Infantry Division	MajGen R. Baltzer
Eberhard Brigade	MajGen Eberhard
21st Corps	*LtGen Nikolaus von Falkenhorst*
228th Infantry Division	MajGen H. Suttner
21st Infantry Division	LtGen H.-K. von Both
1st Corps	*LtGen Walter Petzel*
1st Infantry Division	LtGen J. von Kortzfleisch
12th Infantry Division	LtGen L. von der Leyen
Corps Brand	*LtGen Fritz Brand*
Lotzen Brigade	MajGen Offenbacher
Goldap Brigade	Col Notle

Army Group South	**ColGen Gerd Von Rundstedt**
239th Infantry Division	MajGen F. Neuling
221st Infantry Division	LtGen J. Pflugbeil
213th Infantry Division	MajGen R. de L'Homme de Courbiere
62nd Infantry Division	MajGen W. Keiner
68th Infantry Division	Col G. Braun
27th Infantry Division	LtGen F. Bergmann

Eighth Army	**Gen der Infanterie Johannes Blaskowitz**
10th Corps	*Gen der Artillerie Wilhelm Ulex*
24th Infantry Division	LtGen F. Olbricht
30th Infantry Division	MajGen K. von Briesen
13th Corps	*Gen der Cavalerie Maximilian Fhr. Weichs*
10th Infantry Division	LtGen C. von Cochenhausen
17th Infantry Division	MajGen H. Loch

Tenth Army	**Gen der Artillerie Walter Von Reichenau**
3rd Light Division	MajGen A. Kuntzen
1st Light Division	MajGen F.W. von Loeper
11th Corps	*Gen der Artillerie Emil Leeb*
18th Infantry Division	MajGen F.K. Cranz
19th Infantry Division	LtGen G. Schwantes
16th Corps	*Gen der Cavalerie Erich Hoepner*
4th Panzer Division	LtGen G.H. Reinhardt
1st Panzer Division	LtGen R. Schmidt
14th Infantry Division	LtGen P. Weyer
31st Infantry Division	LtGen R. Kaempfe
4th Corps	*Gen der Infanterie Viktor von Schwedler*
46th Infantry Division	MajGen P. von Hase
4th Infantry Division	MajGen E. Hansen
15th Corps	*Gen der Infanterie Hermann Hoth*
2nd Light Division	LtGen G. Stumme
14th Corps	*Gen der Infanterie Gustav von Wietersheim*
13th Motorised Division	LtGen M. von Faber du Faur
29th Motorised Division	LtGen J. Lemelsen

Fourteenth Army	**ColGen Wilhelm List**
22nd Corps	*Gen der Cavalerie Ewald Von Kleist*
1st Mountain Division	MajGen L. Kubler
2nd Mountain Division	LtGen V. Fuerstein
8th Corps	*Gen der Infanterie Ernst Busch*
8th Infantry Division	LtGen R. Koch-Erpach
28th Infantry Division	LtGen H. von Obstfelder
5th Panzer Division	LtGen H. von Vietinghoff
17th Corps	*Gen der Infanterie Werner Kienitz*
44th Infantry Division	LtGen A. Schubert
45th Infantry Division	LtGen F. Materna
7th Infantry Division	MajGen E. Ott
18th Corps	*Gen der Infanterie Baier*
2nd Panzer Division	LtGen R. Veiel
4th Light Division	MajGen A. Hubicki
3rd Mountain Division	MajGen E. Dietl

(Slovak) Army Group Bernolak	
1st Janosik Division	Col A. Pulanich
2nd Skultety Division	Gen A. Cunderlik
3rd Razus Division	LtCol A. Malar
Mobile Group Kalinciak	LtCol J. Imro

THE CAMPAIGN

Opening Moves – Mobilisation and Provocations

Hitler had planned to initiate the war on 26 August 1939 and German forces began to move to their start lines the afternoon before. The announcement of the Anglo-Polish security pact on the afternoon of 25 August 1939 left Hitler considerably shaken, however, and he ordered the army to postpone the attack while further diplomatic ventures with Italy were pursued. Not all units received the message and there were a number of small border incidents, including an attempt by a Brandenburger unit to seize a rail junction and tunnel in the key Jablonka pass leading through the southern Carpathian mountains. German guerrilla units in western Poland stepped up their sabotage activity, and the Luftwaffe continued their high-altitude reconnaissance flights over Poland. Although the Poles spotted the aircraft, there was little they could do as their obsolete fighters could not reach the high altitudes of the specialised German reconnaissance aircraft.

The Poles had mobilised 700,000 troops by late August, but they had been constrained from ordering a full-scale mobilisation by pressure

The Kriegsmarine moved the old battleship *Schleswig-Holstein* into Danzig in late August. It is usually credited with firing the opening shot of the war when it began bombarding the Polish garrison on Westerplatte in the early hours of 1 September 1939. (NARA)

The Poles had a few government buildings in the free city of Danzig under international treaty, the most prominent of which was the post office. Polish buildings were attacked by local German paramilitary units including the SS-Heimwehr, which was equipped with some of the 14 ex-Austrian Steyr ADGZ M35 armoured cars. (NARA)

from France and Britain. The Western powers were haunted by dark memories of how the mobilisations of 1914 had set the First World War in motion, but drew questionable conclusions from their historical experience. German activity across the frontier made it clear to the Poles that their neighbours were planning military action and Marshal Rydz-Smigly ordered full mobilisation on 30 August. In spite of the ominous situation on the frontier, the French embassy pressured Marshal Rydz-Smigly to rescind the call-up. The Polish government realised that British and French military support was their only hope of successfully resisting a German attack, and reluctantly agreed again.

German Panzer units in Poland were equipped mainly with light tanks like the PzKpfw II, seen here armed with a 20mm cannon. It is followed by several PzKpfw I including the radio-equipped BefehlsPanzer I command type. (NARA)

Poland's small fleet of ships would be of little use in what increasingly appeared to be the inevitable war with Germany, so the fleet was dispersed from its ports. On 30 August, Operation Pekin was put into motion and the destroyer flotilla was dispatched to Britain in time to clear the Danish straits before war broke out.

By 31 August, the situation along the borders became so grave that Rydz-Smigly again ordered full mobilisation in spite of continuing British and French pressure to refrain from doing so. However, the delayed and confused mobilisation served only to make Poland's precarious situation worse. While the Wehrmacht was able to attack in a fully mobilised condition, the Polish army had been able to mobilise only about 65 per cent of its strength before the war broke out, with many of the reservists in transit when Germany struck.

Hitler continued to hope that the Western powers would refrain from aiding the Poles, and so concocted a pretext to try to shift the blame on to the Poles. Under Operation Himmler, SS troops in Polish uniforms staged a phoney attack on the radio station in the border town of Gleiwitz and broadcast inflammatory messages to the Polish minority in eastern Germany to take up arms against Hitler. The bodies of some concentration camp victims dressed in Polish uniforms were left behind as further evidence of Polish aggression for the benefit of foreign journalists brought to the scene. The amateurish charade fooled nobody and Europe grimly braced itself for war.

THE GERMAN ATTACK

The war was scheduled to start at 0445hrs, but in fact began around 0400hrs when the old battleship *Schleswig-Holstein* slipped its moorings in Danzig and began a bombardment of the neighbouring Polish transit base on Westerplatte. Due to treaty restrictions, the Poles were forbidden from fortifying the peninsula, but in fact had reinforced the walls of many buildings. As a result, the small garrison was able to hold out for a week in spite of intense bombardment and repeated infantry assaults. Westerplatte was sometimes called the 'Polish Verdun' due to the horrendous pounding the tenacious defenders received during the first week of fighting.

The remnants of the Polish fleet were smothered by German air attack. The submarine flotilla dispersed into the Baltic to lay mines and hunt for coastal transports, while the only remaining major surface combatants – the destroyer *Wicher* and the minelayer *Gryf* – began mine-laying operations off the coast. The small naval air detachment was wiped out in air raids during the first few days of fighting. On 3 September, the Kriegsmarine sent two destroyers towards the Polish naval facilities, but they were damaged by gunfire from the coastal guns at Hel and gunfire from *Wicher* and *Gryf*. The Luftwaffe responded with a highly effective air raid, which sank Poland's two remaining major warships. The smaller coastal minelayers escaped the air raids until 16 September when they were finally sunk.

Fighting in the port city of Danzig was conducted by paramilitary units on both sides and was especially savage. Workers in the Polish post office barricaded the building but were eventually overwhelmed by the

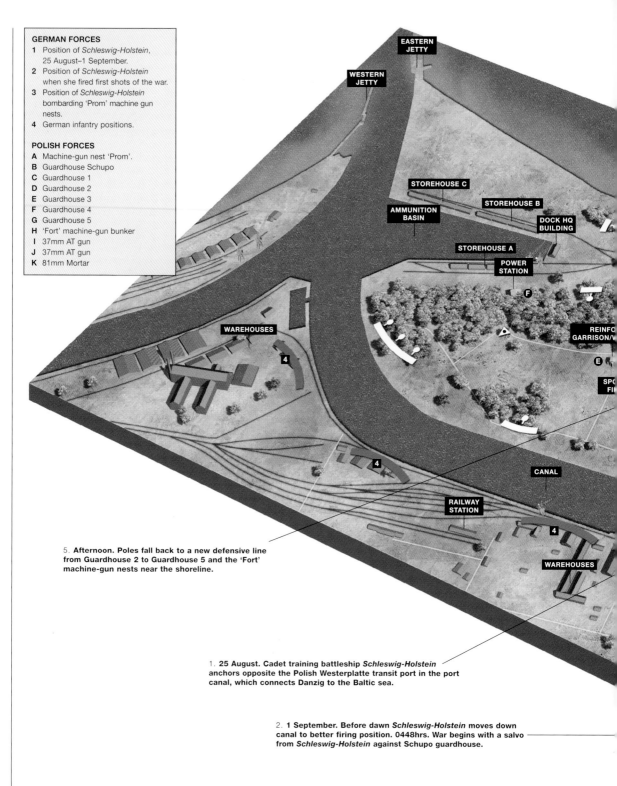

GERMAN FORCES
1 Position of *Schleswig-Holstein*, 25 August–1 September.
2 Position of *Schleswig-Holstein* when she fired first shots of the war.
3 Position of *Schleswig-Holstein* bombarding 'Prom' machine gun nests.
4 German infantry positions.

POLISH FORCES
A Machine-gun nest 'Prom'.
B Guardhouse Schupo
C Guardhouse 1
D Guardhouse 2
E Guardhouse 3
F Guardhouse 4
G Guardhouse 5
H 'Fort' machine-gun bunker
I 37mm AT gun
J 37mm AT gun
K 81mm Mortar

EASTERN JETTY

WESTERN JETTY

STOREHOUSE C

AMMUNITION BASIN

STOREHOUSE B

DOCK HQ BUILDING

STOREHOUSE A

POWER STATION

F

REINFO GARRISON/V

E

SP FI

WAREHOUSES

4

4

CANAL

RAILWAY STATION

4

WAREHOUSES

5. **Afternoon. Poles fall back to a new defensive line from Guardhouse 2 to Guardhouse 5 and the 'Fort' machine-gun nests near the shoreline.**

1. **25 August. Cadet training battleship *Schleswig-Holstein* anchors opposite the Polish Westerplatte transit port in the port canal, which connects Danzig to the Baltic sea.**

2. **1 September. Before dawn *Schleswig-Holstein* moves down canal to better firing position. 0448hrs. War begins with a salvo from *Schleswig-Holstein* against Schupo guardhouse.**

DEFENSE OF WESTERPLATTE

1–7 September 1939, viewed from the southeast, showing the initial bombardment by the German battleship *Schleswig-Holstein* and the Polish garrison's week-long resistance under intense artillery and air attack and repeated infantry assaults.

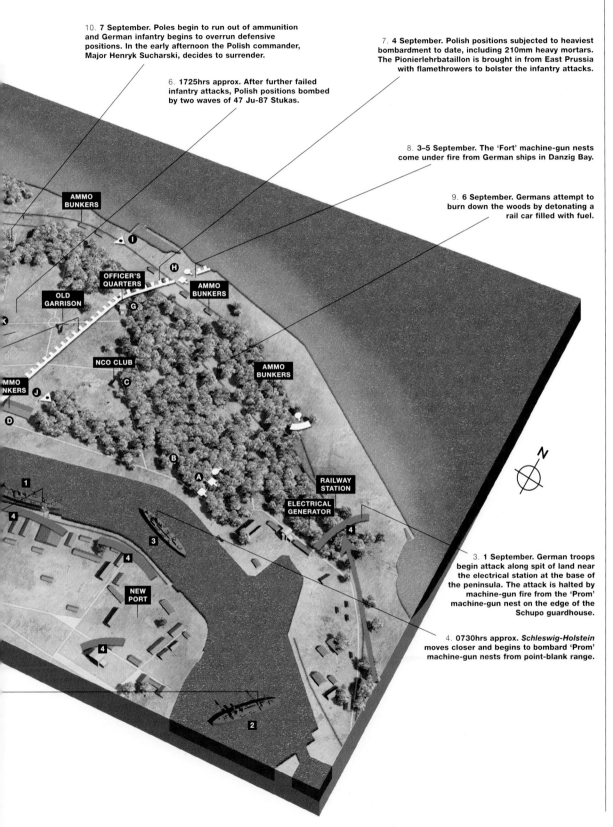

10. **7 September.** Poles begin to run out of ammunition and German infantry begins to overrun defensive positions. In the early afternoon the Polish commander, Major Henryk Sucharski, decides to surrender.

6. **1725hrs approx.** After further failed infantry attacks, Polish positions bombed by two waves of 47 Ju-87 Stukas.

7. **4 September.** Polish positions subjected to heaviest bombardment to date, including 210mm heavy mortars. The Pionierlehrbataillon is brought in from East Prussia with flamethrowers to bolster the infantry attacks.

8. **3–5 September.** The 'Fort' machine-gun nests come under fire from German ships in Danzig Bay.

9. **6 September.** Germans attempt to burn down the woods by detonating a rail car filled with fuel.

AMMO
BUNKERS

I

OFFICER'S
QUARTERS

H

OLD
GARRISON

G

AMMO
BUNKERS

K

NCO CLUB

C

AMMO
BUNKERS

MMO
NKERS

J

D

B

A

RAILWAY
STATION

ELECTRICAL
GENERATOR

1

4

3

4

4

4

NEW
PORT

4

2

N

3. **1 September.** German troops begin attack along spit of land near the electrical station at the base of the peninsula. The attack is halted by machine-gun fire from the 'Prom' machine-gun nest on the edge of the Schupo guardhouse.

4. **0730hrs approx.** *Schleswig-Holstein* moves closer and begins to bombard 'Prom' machine-gun nests from point-blank range.

SS Heimwehr Danzig supported by marines and paramilitary units. Many of the workers were shot after surrendering.

Luftwaffe operations along the coast were constrained by dense early morning fog in many areas. The initial German attack across the Pomeranian corridor was preceded by efforts to seize key rail bridges and stations along the Chojnice–Tczew line. At 0430hrs, Stukas from 3/1 Stuka Geschwader bombed the key Tczew bridge in the Pomeranian corridor, hoping to disarm the demolition charges, but the mission failed. The Wehrmacht then attempted to sneak several armoured assault cars into the station behind the daily civilian transit train. However, the Poles were ready, having been alerted by the premature Stuka attack, and they set off the demolition charges, dropping the bridge. The attack on Chojnice was spearheaded by an armoured train but was beaten back.

The Polish forces of Army Pomorze in the Pomeranian corridor consisted of two infantry divisions and a cavalry brigade. Their deployment was more political than tactical, since Warsaw feared that the Germans might attempt to seize the corridor as they had the Sudetenland in actions short of a full-scale war. The Polish units were positioned to make sure that any German actions would by resisted. Once full-scale war broke out and the German Fourth Army began its assault, their political mission became moot, and they began a fighting withdrawal southward to more defensible positions. In the rearguard, the Pomorska Cavalry Brigade fought a day-long series of engagements with the German 20th Motorised Infantry Division along the Brda Rivers, prompting the German commander to request permission to withdraw 'before intense cavalry pressure'. In the late afternoon, the commander of the 18th Lancer regiment, Col K. Mastelarz, led two understrength squadrons in a raid behind the lines. Galloping out of the forest, they caught a German infantry battalion in the open and mounted a successful sabre charge that decimated the startled German formation. Towards the end of the skirmish, several German armoured cars arrived and began firing at the mounted troops. About 20 troopers

The PzKpfw I did not prove very durable in combat. Its armour could be easily penetrated by Polish anti-tank rifles or 37mm anti-tank guns. This one apparently fell victim to a 75mm field gun, which were often used in the direct-fire role for anti-tank defence. A total of 89 were lost in the 1939 fighting. (J. Magnuski)

The most potent anti-tank weapon in Polish service in 1939 was the wz. 36 37mm anti-tank gun, a licence-manufactured version of the Swedish Bofors design. There were 27 in each infantry division and 14 in each cavalry brigade, with about 1,200 in service in 1939. (Pilsudski Institute)

were killed including the commander before the cavalry could withdraw. The following day, Italian war correspondents were brought to the scene and were told that the troopers had been killed while charging tanks. The story became more embellished with every retelling, becoming a staple of German propaganda and the most enduring myth of the Polish campaign. In spite of the cavalry's defence, the 3rd Panzer Division was able to secure an unopposed crossing over the Brda Rivers.

While the Fourth Army was fighting its way across the Pomeranian corridor, the German Third Army in East Prussia began the first attacks southward towards Warsaw. Two corps began the assault, which soon became entangled in the Mlawa fortification line. Mlawa was one of the few locations with any significant modern fortifications, as it was the obvious approach route to Warsaw from the north. Two German divisions of the 1st Corps conducted the assault with the support of tanks from the Kempf Panzer Division. Manned by the Polish 20th Infantry Division, the fortifications held out against repeated assaults. In the meantime, the Wodrig Corps attempted to skirt around the Mlawa defences to the east, attacking the right wing of the 20th Infantry Division with two infantry divisions. However, the fortifications were situated with swampy ground on either side. Curiously enough, the defensive positions of the Mazowiecka Cavalry Brigade along the Ulatkowka River were attacked by the sole German cavalry unit, the 1st Cavalry Brigade, in one of the few cavalry-versus-cavalry battles of the war. While there were some skirmishes between mounted patrols, most of the fighting was dismounted. By the end of the first day of fighting, the German Third Army was stalled.

The driving force in the Wehrmacht's assault on Poland was Rundstedt's Army Group South, especially its two northern elements, the Eight and Tenth Armies in Silesia. These formations were intended to crash through the opposing Army Lodz and Army Krakow, cross the Warta River, envelope the Polish forces along the western frontier and drive on Warsaw. As a result, these two armies had a disproportionate

CAVALRY DEFENSE AT MOKRA, 1 SEPTEMBER 1939
(pages 44–45)

Although the myth of Polish cavalry charging German Panzers has dominated the popular image of the 1939 campaign, the actual combat record was considerably different. The most dramatic encounter between cavalry and Panzers took place on the first day of the campaign when the Wolynian Cavalry Brigade confronted the 4th Panzer Division near the small village of Mokra. The resulting battle was a reminder of the high morale and excellent training of the Polish cavalry, but also of their limitations in contemporary combat. Polish defences at Mokra hinged on the two principal types of anti-tank weapons: anti-tank rifles and the Bofors 37mm anti-tank gun. The scene here shows one of the Bofors 37mm anti-tank guns in action (1). This small weapon was license-produced in Poland, and was capable of knocking out any contemporary German tank. Defending the Bofors from German infantry is a squad automatic weapons gunner to the right (2). The standard Polish squad automatic weapon in the campaign was a license copy of the Browning Automatic Rifle, familiar to US infantry as the BAR.

During the afternoon fighting around Mokra, the German Panzer companies managed to break through the forward Polish defences, and a few infiltrated as far as the railway line running behind the village. The Wolynian Cavalry Brigade was supported by Armoured Train 53 *Smialy* (3), and the Panzers

were taken under fire at close range, with several Panzers being knocked out (4). These trains had two artillery cars (5), each armed with two turreted guns and several machine guns. They also had an assault company of infantry in a special armoured car, and a few tankettes on special flat-cars that could disembark for scouting or attack. Armoured trains had played a prominent role in the fighting on the eastern front in World War I, and were especially important in the Russian Civil War and the related conflicts such as the 1920 Russo-Polish War. They provided a unique blend of mobility, protection, and firepower compared to the road-bound armoured cars of the day. They were used by both the German and Polish forces in 1939, though their day had passed. Although effective in some battles such as Mokra, they were extremely vulnerable to air attack, and *Smialy* was damaged on 1 September during an air attack.

In 1939, Blitzkrieg was still in its infancy, and the German attack at Mokra demonstrated the need for further refinement of Panzer division tactics. The early Panzer divisions lacked the infantry necessary to overcome a determined, prepared defence like the Polish defence at Mokra. In the future, the Wehrmacht would rely on their infantry divisions to effect the breakthrough, and use the superior mobility of the Panzer divisions to exploit the breakthrough as the 4th Panzer Division would demonstrate a few days later in the race for Warsaw. (Howard Gerrard)

Armoured Train No.53 *Smialy* supported Army Lodz in the border battles and took part in the fighting with 4th Panzer Division near Mokra on 1 September. It had two armoured gun carriages like this one, each with two turreted wz. 02/26 75mm guns. These guns were effective against the thinly armoured German tanks, but the trains were vulnerable to Stuka attack. (J. Magnuski)

share of the Panzer and light divisions. The opening phase was largely uneventful, as the main Polish defensive line was in the scattered forests about 32km (20 miles) from the frontier. The most intense battle in this sector occurred around the village of Mokra, which was held by the Wolynska Cavalry Brigade. Despite repeated attacks by the 4th Panzer Division during the day, the cavalry held its ground and inflicted significant losses. The German tank attacks were poorly co-ordinated with the accompanying infantry; a reflection of the novelty of massed tank operations and the difficulty of putting the new doctrine into practice. At least one of the German attacks was repulsed with the assistance of the armoured train *Smialy* in one of several encounters between Panzers and armoured trains during the campaign. Stuka attacks against the brigade's rear area caused serious losses of horses and supplies, but were unsuccessful in breaking Polish resistance. If the defence of Mokra was proof of the excellent training and morale of the cavalry, it was also evidence of its shortcomings in contemporary conflict. Casualties were so high that the brigade was forced to withdraw that evening, with the 4th Panzer Division on its heels.

The Germans had greater success against Army Krakow to the south. Army Krakow had one of the most difficult tasks of the Polish higher formations, facing the heaviest concentration of German divisions including most of its mechanised forces; four Panzer divisions and four light divisions. In addition, its sector spanned an area from the Upper Silesian industrial region to the Carpathian foothills in the south. While the Wolynska Cavalry Brigade was preoccupied with the main assault against its positions around Mokra, the 1st Panzer Division drove a wedge between it and the Polish 7th Infantry Division to its south. This division was attacked frontally by the German 46th Infantry Division, and its southern flank was threatened when the 2nd Light Division pushed into the defences of the Krakowska Cavalry Brigade. Two more German infantry divisions were ready to reinforce the assault on the hapless 7th Infantry Division. Less progress was enjoyed to the south when the 8th and 239th Infantry Divisions assaulted the fortified zone around the

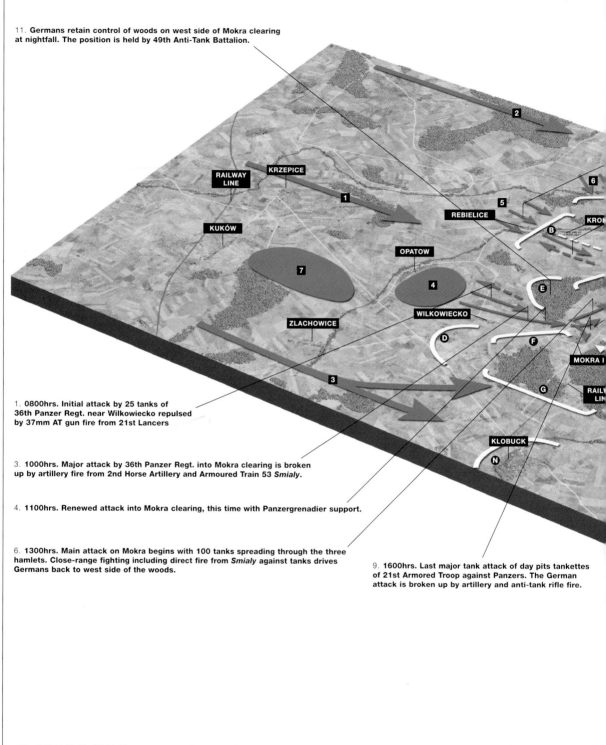

11. Germans retain control of woods on west side of Mokra clearing at nightfall. The position is held by 49th Anti-Tank Battalion.

RAILWAY LINE

KRZEPICE

1

2

6

5

REBIELICE

KRO

KUKÓW

OPATOW

B

7

4

E

ZLACHOWICE

WILKOWIECKO

D

F

3

MOKRA I

G

RAIL LI

KLOBUCK

N

1. 0800hrs. Initial attack by 25 tanks of 36th Panzer Regt. near Wilkowiecko repulsed by 37mm AT gun fire from 21st Lancers

3. 1000hrs. Major attack by 36th Panzer Regt. into Mokra clearing is broken up by artillery fire from 2nd Horse Artillery and Armoured Train 53 Smialy.

4. 1100hrs. Renewed attack into Mokra clearing, this time with Panzergrenadier support.

6. 1300hrs. Main attack on Mokra begins with 100 tanks spreading through the three hamlets. Close-range fighting including direct fire from Smialy against tanks drives Germans back to west side of the woods.

9. 1600hrs. Last major tank attack of day pits tankettes of 21st Armored Troop against Panzers. The German attack is broken up by artillery and anti-tank rifle fire.

CAVALRY vs. ARMOUR AT MOKRA

1 September 1939, viewed from the southeast, showing the repeated attacks by the 4th Panzer Division around the village of Mokra on the Wolynska Cavalry Brigade, which determinedly holds its ground, inflicting significant losses on the poorly coordinated tank and infantry attacks.

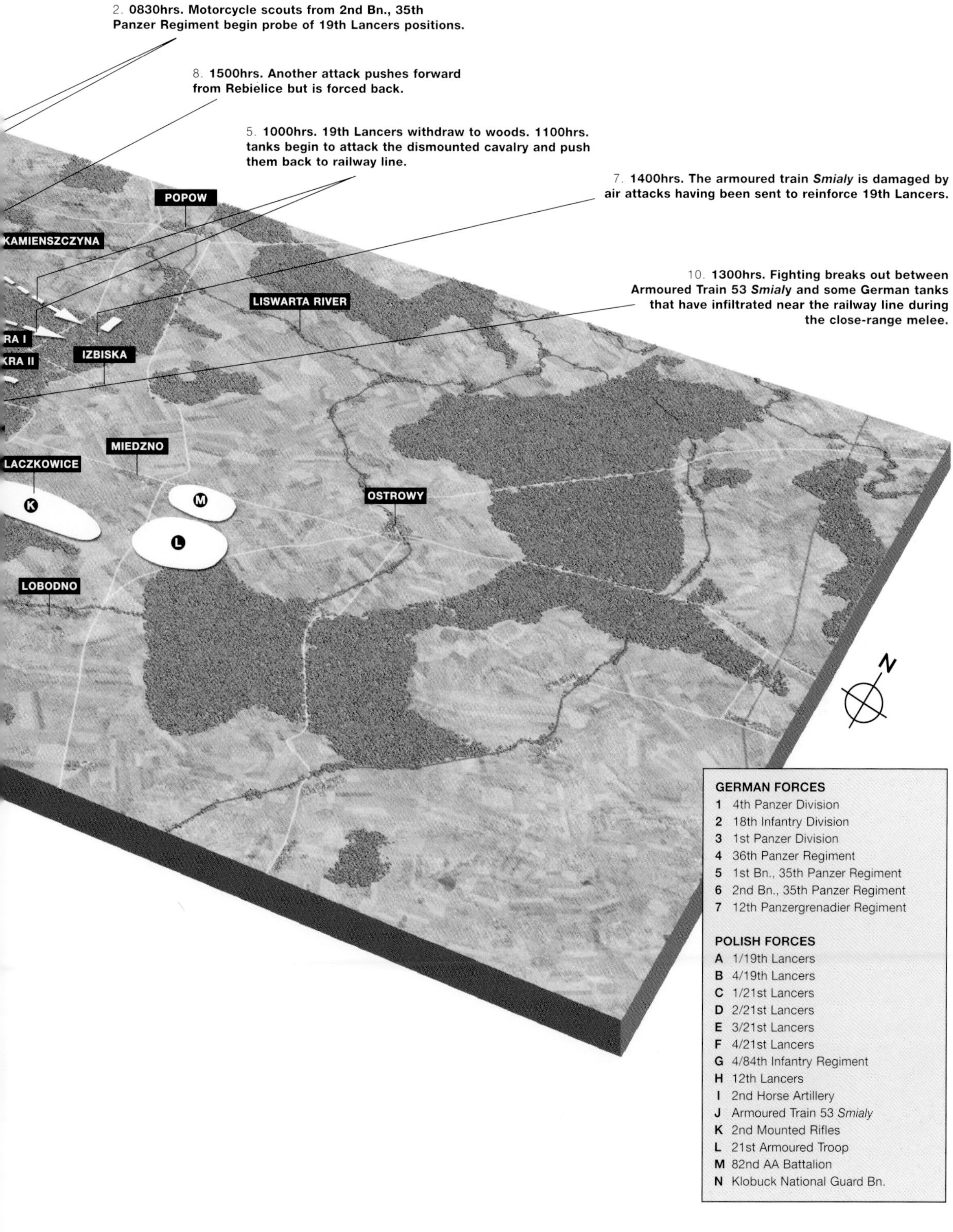

2. **0830hrs. Motorcycle scouts from 2nd Bn., 35th Panzer Regiment begin probe of 19th Lancers positions.**

8. **1500hrs. Another attack pushes forward from Rebielice but is forced back.**

5. **1000hrs. 19th Lancers withdraw to woods. 1100hrs. tanks begin to attack the dismounted cavalry and push them back to railway line.**

7. **1400hrs. The armoured train Smiały is damaged by air attacks having been sent to reinforce 19th Lancers.**

10. **1300hrs. Fighting breaks out between Armoured Train 53 Smiały and some German tanks that have infiltrated near the railway line during the close-range melee.**

POPOW

KAMIENSZCZYNA

LISWARTA RIVER

RA I
RA II

IZBISKA

MIEDZNO

LACZKOWICE

K

M

OSTROWY

L

LOBODNO

N

GERMAN FORCES
1 4th Panzer Division
2 18th Infantry Division
3 1st Panzer Division
4 36th Panzer Regiment
5 1st Bn., 35th Panzer Regiment
6 2nd Bn., 35th Panzer Regiment
7 12th Panzergrenadier Regiment

POLISH FORCES
A 1/19th Lancers
B 4/19th Lancers
C 1/21st Lancers
D 2/21st Lancers
E 3/21st Lancers
F 4/21st Lancers
G 4/84th Infantry Regiment
H 12th Lancers
I 2nd Horse Artillery
J Armoured Train 53 Smiały
K 2nd Mounted Rifles
L 21st Armoured Troop
M 82nd AA Battalion
N Klobuck National Guard Bn.

industrial city of Katowice. The neighbouring 28th Infantry Division and 5th Panzer Division struck the Polish 55th and 6th Infantry Divisions.

Aside from the regular military operations, there was considerable turmoil in the rear areas due to the operations of German guerrilla units that had been formed prior to the war by the Abwehr (Military Intelligence). Silesia had a sizeable pro-Nazi German minority and there were numerous small-scale skirmishes between regular Polish army units, police and German guerrilla groups.

The 22nd Panzer Corps, operating out of Slovakia, began a determined attack on Polish mountain defences along the Dunajec River. The 2nd Panzer Division manoeuvred its way past the Polish Dunajec line, held mainly by KOP border troops, obliging Army Krakow to commit its mechanised reserve, the 10th Mechanised Brigade. The German advance was finally stopped later in the day when reinforcements arrived in the shape of units of the Polish 6th Infantry Division. The German 1st and 2nd Mountain Divisions, supported by Slovak units, began attempts to cross the Carpathian mountains in the Army Karpaty sector. No serious gains were made on 1 September due to the difficulty of the terrain.

Air operations

The Luftwaffe's doctrine focused on the need to gain air superiority over its enemies. Consequently, more than half of the Luftwaffe's missions on the first day of the war against Poland were staged against Polish airfields. One of the myths of the September campaign was that the Polish Air Force was destroyed on its fields on 1 September 1939. In fact the air force dispersed to improvised air strips on 31 August. The Luftwaffe was also hampered in its initial strikes on the morning of 1 September due to fog and mist. The only airfield attacked in force, Rakowice near Krakow, lost 28 unserviceable aircraft that could not be flown out the day before. While the dispersion saved the Polish aircraft from the initial German attack, it also made operations more difficult since the units were operating out of grass strips with limited technical support. The Luftwaffe had considerable trouble locating the dispersed Polish bases, and only about 24 combat aircraft were destroyed on the ground during the campaign, though many unserviceable aircraft and trainers were destroyed. Other Luftwaffe missions were directed against a wide variety of objectives, including key road and rail targets. These were not close-air support missions but rather attacks on targets selected prior to the outbreak of the war. In 1939, the Luftwaffe was not yet prepared, either in terms of doctrine or communication equipment, to carry out close air support missions on demand from the army.

After the first few days of air attacks against Polish airfields, the Luftwaffe began to shift more of its operations to missions supporting the ground forces. Once again, these were not close air support missions as has often been reported, but rather targets selected by the air staff. The Luftwaffe was highly effective in interdicting Polish troop movements along road and rail lines, which further complicated the already confused mobilisation of reserves. Attempts to use the Luftwaffe in direct close support of ground operations did take place later in the campaign, notably the attacks against the Bzura counter-offensive in the second week of the war and the attacks on Warsaw in late September.

The symbol of Blitzkrieg was the Junkers Ju-87 Stuka dive-bomber. Against relatively modest air opposition in Poland, they proved very effective in bombing communication lines and other targets. When faced with stiffer opposition, as in the Battle of Britain in 1940, their value quickly plummeted as they proved to be slow and vulnerable to modern fighters. (NARA)

The Luftwaffe ruled the skies if for no other reason than its vastly superior size. The Polish air force on 1 September had a front-line strength of only 397 combat aircraft, while the Luftwaffe had more than five times this number, the majority of which were considerably more modern. The only area where the Luftwaffe met serious resistance was around Warsaw. Goering planned a major air attack on Warsaw on the first day of the war, codenamed *Wasserkante*. However, the attack was something of a shambles due to low-lying clouds. The four bomber groups that arrived over the city were confronted by the Pursuit Brigade and the Polish fighters shot down 16 aircraft at a cost of ten fighters lost and 24 damaged during the course of the day's fighting. The Pursuit Brigade was undoubtedly the most effective element of the air force, credited with 42 German aircraft in the first six days of the war. However, these modest losses did little to stop the repeated German attacks and the Luftwaffe could roam at will over most of the country. By the evening of

Although less heralded than the Stuka, the sturdy Henschel Hs-126 army co-operation aircraft was a frequent hazard to Polish infantry units since it was used for aerial reconnaissance and artillery spotting. The Polish PZL P.23 Karas was designed for a similar role. (NARA)

6 September, the Pursuit Brigade had lost 38 of its 54 fighters, and was transferred east to Lublin. After this, the defence of the capital fell to anti-aircraft guns alone. Other fighter squadrons flew with the army's air force, which was attached to the field armies, and these squadrons were involved in numerous air battles with German combat aircraft through the first week of the war. Of the 285 German aircraft shot down during the Polish campaign, at least 126 were shot down by Polish fighters. A further 279 German aircraft suffered significant damage.

The Polish Bomber Brigade was less successful in its missions than the Pursuit Brigade, as their most significant element, the new *Los* bomber squadrons, had only recently converted to the type and were still working up when the war began. The first major bombing mission was conducted by 24 P.23 *Karas* light bombers against the armoured spearheads of the German Tenth Army on 2 September. Unlike the Stuka, which was designed as a dedicated bomber, bombing was only a secondary function for the *Karas*. They had to attack the Panzer formations from low altitude in level flight at relatively slow speeds, making them vulnerable to German 20mm anti-aircraft guns. The Polish pilots pressed home their attacks with considerable courage, but their

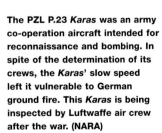

The most modern aircraft in Polish service in 1939 was the excellent PZL P.37 *Los* medium bomber. Plans to use it to conduct missions into Germany were cancelled, and it was used on a number of occasions in risky low-altitude missions against German spearheads moving on Warsaw. (Pilsudski Institute)

losses were high. The more modern *Los* medium bombers were first committed in strength on 3 September, again attacking the armoured spearheads of Tenth Army. The attacks continued over the next few days; however, some ten *Los* bombers were lost to flak on 4 September alone. Although the Poles believed they had inflicted serious losses, there is little evidence that the attacks impeded the armoured assault. On 7 September, the Bomber Brigade was shifted to the northern front to attack the armoured spearheads of Bock's Army Group North. By this stage, increasing shortages of spare parts and fuel, and the deteriorating maintenance level of the squadrons severely reduced their capabilities. An attempt was made to reinforce the brigade with *Karas* from local army units, but these aircraft were in poor shape after more than a week of fighting and operations from rough grass strips. The *Karas* units deployed in support of the field armies conducted numerous bombing raids. By 6 September, the army air force had lost half its *Karas*. During the campaign, about 260 Polish aircraft were lost to enemy action including about 70 lost in air-to-air combat.

The East Prussian theatre

Army Group North continued its attempts to break across the Pomeranian corridor on 2 September. As planned, the northernmost Polish forces had withdrawn southward, leaving the Seacoast Defence Forces, including the Westerplatte garrison, completely isolated along the Baltic coastline. Much of the fighting in the corridor centred around the Tuchola Forest, with the 3rd Panzer Division managing to push forces across the main branch of the Brda River, nearly behind the Polish defensive line. From East Prussia itself, two German infantry divisions attempted to penetrate the eastern side of the corridor against two Polish infantry divisions, but with little success. By the end of the day, the two Polish infantry divisions and cavalry brigade were nearly trapped. In the fighting on 3 September, the 27th Division was able to fight its way southward to Bydgoszcz, but the other units remained encircled and suffered heavy casualties in the fighting. Anticipating the fall of Bydgoszcz, German insurgents prematurely staged an armed uprising at 1000hrs on 3 September, but they were routed by Polish militia forces backed by the army. In mid-afternoon, Army Pomorze was ordered to withdraw to the main defensive line behind the Vistula. This

The Polish Westerplatte transit garrison on a peninsula on the outskirts of Danzig was one of the first German objectives during the campaign. It was pulverised at point-blank range by the heavy guns of the *Schleswig-Holstein*, leading to its nickname, the 'Polish Verdun'. The Polish garrison had secretly reinforced several of the buildings with concrete, so they were able to hold out for seven days against repeated German attacks. The results of the bombardment are evident in this photo taken shortly after the surrender. (NARA)

was due not to particular difficulties in Pomerania, but to the collapse of the Mlawa defences to the east. In total the Poles lost about 10,000 troops in the Pomeranian fighting, mainly the units trapped in the corridor. With the Polish defences evaporating, Army Group North began transferring forces from Germany into East Prussia for the main assault against Warsaw. The 10th Panzer Division was one of the first major units sent across the corridor.

Continued German assaults on the fortified positions of the 20th Infantry Division near Mlawa had proved futile, so greater effort was made to outflank the defences to the east. The Kempf Panzer Division began to make inroads into the defences of the badly overextended Mazowiecka Cavalry Brigade. Even the commitment of the 8th Infantry Division could not restrain the German advance now. By late afternoon on 2 September, the Polish defensive line had been substantially ruptured in this sector, and Army Modlin was ordered to withdraw southward to the main Vistula line. One of the more curious operations during these frontier battles was the raid into East Prussia by the Podlaska Cavalry Brigade on the evening of 2/3 September along a quiet eastern sector of the East Prussian front. The raid was the only Polish operation on German soil; and there were even a few small clashes with German territorial Landwehr units before the Poles withdrew. Elements of the 20th Infantry continued to hold out in Mlawa, hoping to slow the German advance. However, by the end of the first week, the Wehrmacht had considerably increased its strength in East Prussia by shifting units from Germany through the corridor.

The Polish forces withdrew towards the fortified garrison town of Modlin. The Kempf Panzer Division managed to cross the Narew River near Rozan on 5 September in spite of the opposition of the 41st Infantry Division. The breach of the defences was widened the next day with another river crossing at Pultusk. Polish counter-attacks failed and Marshal Rydz-Smigly ordered Army Modlin to retreat once again, this time over the San River. As in the case of the Mlawa fortifications, the Modlin garrison continued to hold out even though it was surrounded.

THE SILESIAN BREAKTHROUGH

Since the German plan called for an encirclement of the Polish forces in western Poland, Bock's Army Group North and Rundstedt's Army Group South were separated from one another by Pomerania. General T. Kutrzeba's Army Poznan was isolated in this region; its original political mission had been to prevent an uncontested German seizure of this disputed border region. There was little fighting in this area for the first three days of the war. Kutrzeba, who had been heavily involved in pre-war planning, was well aware that the Germans were making their main thrusts around his formation. Communications with Warsaw were finally restored on 3 September, and Kutrzeba vehemently argued that his forces should begin operations against the northern flank of Rundstedt's command, namely against Blaskowitz's Eighth Army. Marshal Rydz-Smigly refused, arguing that it would lead to their premature destruction. Rydz-Smigly wanted to avoid a decisive battle on the west bank of the Vistula.

Rundstedt was worried precisely about an attack of the sort proposed by Kutrzeba. In his original planning, Rundstedt had attempted to cover this flank with German cavalry units, but he was told by Hitler to use the

STUKA ATTACK, SEPTEMBER 1939 (pages 56–57)

The Junkers Ju-87B Stuka dive-bomber has remained the icon of Blitzkrieg warfare. The demoralizing howl of the Stuka in its bombing dive terrified soldiers and civilians alike. Here we see an attack by a pair of Junkers Ju-87B Stukas of Stukagruppe 1 (1), which operated out of Elbing in East Prussia. Air attack introduced a third dimension to the modern battlefield, enabling powerful attacks deep behind enemy lines.

Cooperation between the Wehrmacht and Luftwaffe was still in its infancy during the 1939 Poland campaign. Contrary to the popular image of Stukas as a form of close air support, there was a lack of adequate radios and appropriate doctrine for such tactics. Instead, Stukas were used mainly to carry out pre-planned air attacks against selected targets, with the targets generally selected by the Luftwaffe staff, not the Wehrmacht.

During the first days of the campaign, their primary mission was to destroy the small Polish air force, a task made very difficult by the dispersion of Polish aircraft to concealed bases prior to the outbreak of the war. As a result, there were numerous encounters between Polish fighters like the P.11c seen here (2), and the attacking Luftwaffe squadrons. The PZL P.11c had been a formidable fighter when it first entered service in the early 1930s. Its monoplane gull-wing design was

advanced for its day when many other air forces, including both Britain and Germany, were still relying on bi-plane fighters. Unfortunately, the Polish budget did not match its defence needs. Polish plans to introduce a modern fighter with an enclosed cockpit and retractable landing gear, the PZL P.50 *Jastrzeb*, failed to materialize in time due to a lack of funds. A single prototype was completed and flew in 1939, but the fighter force depended entirely on aircraft that were a generation behind Germany's. Indeed, the Stuka was as fast as a P.11c and unless careful, Polish fighters could fall victim to a skilled Stuka pilot. In fact one of the first air-to-air battles of the war saw a Stuka shooting down a P.11c in the Krakow area. Heavy combat attrition of the Polish fighter force in the first few days of the campaign gave the Luftwaffe mastery of the air and Stukas were later able to bomb their targets with impunity. They were especially effective in attacking columns of troops and equipment moving to the front, and they helped to disrupt and paralyse Polish reinforcement of their battered defences. By the later stage of the campaign, the Wehrmacht and Luftwaffe began to cooperate in planning Stuka missions, laying the groundwork for the development of true close air support tactics. The Stukas were used with considerable success in the counter-attacks against the Polish Bzura river counter-offensive. (Howard Gerrard)

The Polish Seacoast Defence Force consisted of a number of coastal-gun batteries and bunkers around Oksywie and Hel. The Oksywie garrison held out until 19 September, and the Hel garrison did not surrender until 1 October. One of the four 152mm Bofors batteries emplaced on the Hel peninsula survived the war and has been preserved in the park behind the armed forces museum in Warsaw. (Author)

SS-Leibstandarte instead. Concerned about the SS unit's inexperience and lack of training, he assigned the task to a regular infantry unit (the 30th Infantry Division) instead. However, it was thinly strung out and would have been vulnerable to an attack by Army Poznan. Rundstedt considered the Eighth Army his 'problem child' due to its relatively weak forces and the paucity of mobile forces for flank security.

In spite of these concerns, Rundstedt continued to press his main assault to the north-east through Silesia. The Wolynska Cavalry Brigade succeeded in holding up the 4th Panzer Division in another day of intense fighting on 2 September, but the Polish 7th Infantry Division to the south was in a dire predicament, pitted against the 1st Panzer Division and two infantry divisions. Its withdrawal towards Czestochowa left one bridge over the Warta River open to the 1st Panzer Division, which lost no time in exploiting the gain. The Poles responded by staging one of their largest air attacks of the campaign using their P.23 *Karas* light bombers. Attacks were conducted against both the 1st and 4th Panzer Divisions, but heavy anti-aircraft fire brought down five P.23s, and seven more were lost on landing due to heavy battle damage. Recognising the breach in the Polish defences, the German Tenth Army concentrated its efforts on this sector the next day, committing additional units including the 3rd Light Division. The Krakowska Cavalry Brigade had one of its regiments overwhelmed, and by 4 September, the 7th Infantry Division had been reduced to a couple of battalions. These battles of 2–4 September along the boundaries between Army Lodz and Army Krakow were the most vital consequence of the first few days of fighting because they opened up the gateway to Warsaw. Since the Tenth Army contained the majority of the German mechanised force, the advances in this sector held the greatest potential for deep exploitation. Furthermore, the terrain in the Warsaw direction was mostly flat farmland, ideal for a mechanised advance.

The situation along Army Krakow's southern flank was a little brighter, in no small measure due to the skilful defence by the 10th Mechanised Brigade against the 2nd Panzer Division. Nevertheless, the steady German advances obliged Army Krakow's commander, General A. Szylling, to request permission to begin withdrawing towards

A German motorised column moves through a devastated Polish town. In 1939, motorcycles were widely used in the German army for reconnaissance in conjunction with light-armoured cars like the SdKfz 221, seen further back in the column. (NARA)

the city of Krakow. The mountainous terrain aided in the defence, and an orderly withdrawal prevented the Germans from penetrating the gap between Armies Krakow and Karpaty.

The Polish high command was shocked by the fast pace of the German advance. Polish planners had correctly anticipated that the main German thrust would emanate out of Silesia towards Warsaw, so Army Prusy was deployed as the main strategic reserve along this avenue of attack. Army Prusy consisted of three infantry divisions and a cavalry brigade, but it was not fully concentrated on 3–4 September 1939 due to the delayed mobilisation problems and the effectiveness of the Luftwaffe campaign against lines of communication. The main threat came from the rapid advance of the 4th and 1st Panzer Divisions towards Piotrkow. A disorganised counter-attack was conducted by elements of the Polish 19th Infantry Division near the city on the morning of 5 September, but the Germans employed the mobility of their Panzer units to find the many gaps in the Polish defences. Curiously enough, the Piotrkow fighting involved one of the few significant contacts between Polish and German tanks formations when the Polish 2nd Tank Battalion was committed to the defence of the city. Although the 7TP tanks managed to knock out 17 Panzers, two self-propelled guns and 14 armoured cars for a loss of only two tanks of their own, the Polish armour in the sector was not used in any concentrated form and its effects were inconsequential. In the midst of these critical battles, Gen Kutrzeba continued to push for a commitment of Army Poznan against the northern flank of Army Group South, but was again rebuffed by Rydz-Smigly.

By the evening of 5 September, the boundary between Army Lodz and Army Krakow had been fully ruptured, and Army Prusy was unable to staunch the flow. The two Panzer divisions managed to push through to Piotrkow, but the Tenth Army had also pushed back Army Krakow's northern flank, opening the way to Kielce. The Polish defence of the approaches to Warsaw was on the verge of collapse. On the evening of 5 September, Marshal Rydz-Smigly ordered that Army Lodz, Army Krakow and Army Prusy should begin to withdraw to the east bank of the Vistula, rather than be trapped and destroyed. In addition, Kutrzeba's Army Poznan was ordered eastward to the Vistula before seeing any significant combat.

Although the Poles did not have extensive border fortifications like the Maginot line, they had some modern bunker complexes along major approaches to key cities, such as in Silesia. The most heavily fortified areas were north of Warsaw including the Mlawa defences, and the older and more established Modlin garrison. (NARA)

THE RACE FOR WARSAW, 7 SEPTEMBER 1939

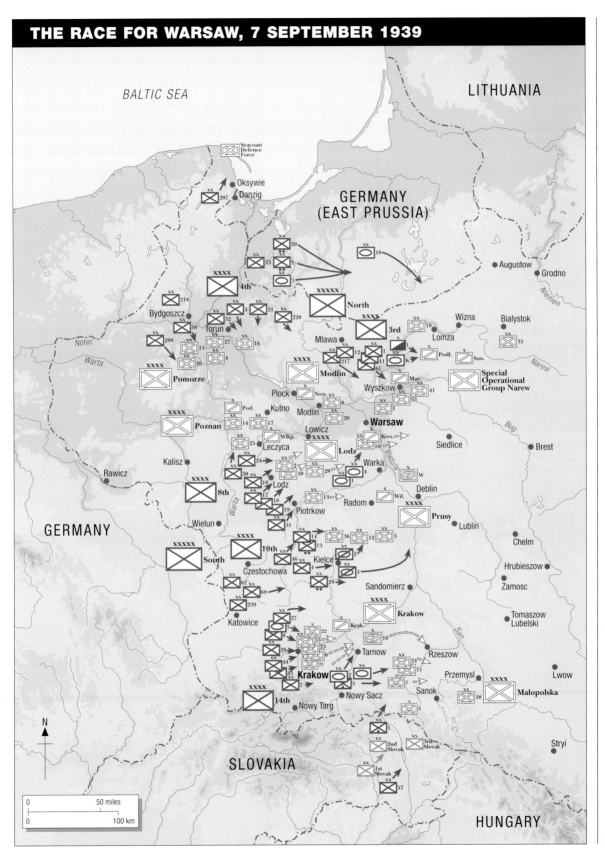

BALTIC SEA

LITHUANIA

GERMANY (EAST PRUSSIA)

GERMANY

SLOVAKIA

HUNGARY

Seacoast Defence Force

Oksywie
Danzig

Augustow
Grodno

Wizna
Bialystok

Lomza

Bydgoszcz
Torun

Mlawa

Notec
Warta

Pomorze

Special Operational Group Narew

Plock
Modlin

Modlin

Wyszkow

Warsaw

Poznan

Kutno
Leczyca
Lowicz

Lodz

Siedlice
Brest

Kalisz

Rawicz

Bug

8th

Lodz

Warka

Deblin

Wielun
Piotrkow

Radom

Prusy

Lublin

Chelm

South

10th

Kielce

Czestochowa

Sandomierz

Hrubieszow
Zamosc

Katowice

Tomaszow
Lubelski

Tarnow

Rzeszow

Krakow

San

Krakow

Przemysl
Lwow

Nowy Sacz
Sanok

Malopolska

14th

Nowy Targ

2nd Slovak
3rd Slovak

Stryi

1st Slovak

N

0   50 miles

0   100 km

North

3rd

Vistula

Narew

Niemen

61

A German artillery unit passes through a Polish village. The lead vehicle is a 3-tonne half-track, towing the standard divisional field gun, the 105mm leFH 18. (NARA)

The situation in the south had become equally bleak, even if not as consequential to overall Polish plans. The German units had finally broken out of the mountains and were pressing hard towards Krakow. The skilful defence of the 10th Mechanised Brigade was eventually overwhelmed by the determined onslaughts of the 2nd Panzer Division and 3rd Mountain Division. On the evening of 5 September, the Polish units were ordered to fall back over the Dunajec River protecting the southern flank of the old capital of Krakow.

By 5 September, both sides began to reassess their plans. The OKH had been hesitant to commit too many of its divisions eastward for fear that they would have to be turned around to respond to a French attack. With no evidence of any French attack developing, this concern began to wane, but had not yet disappeared. To the commanders in the field like Rundstedt, it was becoming clear that the Poles were obviously attempting to avoid a decisive battle on the western bank of the Vistula, exemplified by the continued inactivity of Kutrzeba's Army Poznan. Noting the withdrawal of Polish units from their fronts, the German field commanders were urging a change in the initial plans for Case White, recognising that their units would have to push further east than originally anticipated to envelop and destroy the Polish army. Brauchitsch and OKH remained hesitant at this commitment, still concerned that if units became entangled to the east, they would be difficult to extract in the event of a French offensive. As late as 5 September, Brauchitsch forbade Bock from pushing too far eastward. Brauchitsch changed his position only on 9 September, by which time it was blatantly evident that the Poles were avoiding the German encirclement attempts by withdrawing, while the French activity was limited to a token offensive.

The Polish situation was grim, as there appeared to be little prospect of restraining the main German thrust out of Silesia. More alarmingly, the Germans were advancing faster than the Poles could retreat, and a successful withdrawal to a new defensive line on the Vistula was far from assured. Rydz-Smigly's main objective continued to be the avoidance of a decisive battle on the west banks of the Vistula in order to keep the army in the field until the anticipated French counter-offensive. This of course was based on a serious misunderstanding of French intentions. The failure of the main Polish reserve formation, Army Prusy, led Rydz-Smigly to order the formation of another strategic reserve, Army Lublin, from remaining reserve units. By the evening of 7 September, Rydz-Smigly was convinced that the Germans would surround Warsaw within a week. Since this would isolate him from the armies in the field, he decided to move the high command from Warsaw to Brzesc-nad-Bugiem (Brest-Litovsk). A small staff was left in Warsaw to handle the transition. It was a serious mistake, as Brzesc was not prepared to handle the communications to the field armies. At a critical time in the establishment of the Vistula defence line, co-ordination from the high command was disrupted. Units received contradictory orders from Warsaw and Brzesc, orders often arrived too late or not at all, and some armies were essentially cut off from any contact with the high command.

Of the Polish armies in the field, Army Krakow's position was the most perilous. Late on 7 September, the 5th Panzer Division found an undefended gap through the Holy Cross mountains, and began to move behind the main Polish defensive lines from the north-west. On the other flank, the German 4th Light Division and 45th Infantry Division seized Tarnow on 7 September after the forces of Army Malopolska withdrew from the Nida River line on the night of 6 September against orders. A day-long battle ensued as Army Krakow tried to fight its way out of the noose being quickly tightened around it.

The four other central Polish armies continued to retreat towards the Vistula, but they were alarmed to find that the German mechanised units were outpacing them. The most serious situation existed in the ruptured boundary between Army Lodz and Army Prusy, with both the 1st and 4th Panzer Division racing through the gap towards Warsaw. The situation on the northern front facing Prussia was less dire for the moment, as the Wehrmacht was consolidating the forces that had been shifted eastward through the Pomeranian corridor in anticipation of a major offensive thrust. Counter-attacks by Army Modlin were unsuccessful. Bock had been arguing with the OKH for some time that he be allowed to press the attack further to the east. The advantage of such an attack would be to undermine any Polish attempt to create a defensive line behind the Vistula. The OKH was at first reluctant to allow him to carry out this option, but the debate remained academic as Bock's forces did not launch the renewed offensive on Warsaw until after the first week of the campaign. By then, the OKH was finally beginning to shift its views towards those held by the field commanders, that an eastward thrust would be necessary to finally trap the Polish forces. Rather than push immediately southward along the western bank of the Vistula, Bock's forces would be permitted to thrust down the eastern bank, to threaten Polish defences along the river line.

Inaction in the west

On 3 September, France and Britain declared war on Germany. There was rejoicing on the streets of Warsaw. There was also hope that the

There were a number of tank-versus-tank clashes during the German push towards Warsaw. The 2nd Light Tank Battalion and the partially equipped 3rd Light Tank Battalion, seen here immediately before the war, were both equipped with the 7TP light tank. The 7TP was based on the British Vickers, but with a diesel engine and a Bofors 37mm gun. Polish armoured units gave a good account of themselves, but were too few in number to have much effect. (George Bradford)

declaration would be followed by military action by the Western powers. In fact, the mobilisation of the French army was very slow, while no real plans had been made for any major offensive operations against Germany. In spite of Gamelin's promises to the Poles in May, French strategic planning was defensively oriented. The French army intended to use the shield of the Maginot line to prevent any major German incursion into France. To cover the unprotected north-east flank, France's substantial mechanised forces would be committed to the establishment of a forward defensive line in Belgium along the Dyle River. However, since Belgium had declared its neutrality in 1936, France would wait until the Germans violated Belgian neutrality before moving their mobile formations forward. The French at the time were confident that they could defeat the Germans using a defensive strategy, since they were convinced that the main lesson of the First World War was that defence had become a stronger means of war than offense. Gamelin was in no rush since he expected that the Poles would hold out for three to four months. The French, like the Poles, badly underestimated the pace of the new style of warfare.

Gamelin's assurance to the Poles in May 1939 was cynical posturing with no real intention of major action. The problem was not capability but will. Confined within the straightjacket of France's defensive strategy, in early September, Gamelin informed his British allies that he would not 'discourage' the French army by a hastily planned offensive. The ghosts of the 1914–18 war weighed heavily on French commanders. There was no enthusiasm at all for attempting to initiate a decisive battle with the Germans. The general staff had already prepared plans for an offensive into the Saar in 1938 as one possible option during the Czech crisis. The plans were dusted off as a half-hearted attempt to honour France's commitments to Poland. French units began to move into place on 4 September, and nine divisions began a move into Germany along a 25km (16-mile) front on 7 September. These units took modest casualties, mainly from mines, and advanced 8km (5 miles) to the edge of Germany's partially built Siegfried line. Disturbed by the grim news from Poland, Gamelin ordered the commander of the Saar offensive,

General Pretelat, to halt and go on the defensive on 12 September. The forces were withdrawn on 4 October 1939 after Poland's defeat.

Britain's actions were no bolder. The British Expeditionary Force would not begin to arrive in France for months. The debate in Britain over possible actions was, at times, surreal. The secretary of state for air, Sir Kingsley Wood, condemned calls in the House of Commons for retaliatory air strikes against Germany, reminding his fellow politicians that they were suggesting an attack on private property. British military action was limited to a campaign of leaflet raids on Germany, derided by one Member of Parliament as 'confetti warfare'.

Hitler had hoped that Britain and France would abandon Poland altogether. Their timid response left the Poles to their fate. France threw away one of its great strategic opportunities, as German forces in the west were too thin to repulse any full-scale assault. German officers interviewed about the campaign after the war expressed their firm belief that if France had struck in force in September 1939, its army would have reached the Rhine in a couple of weeks, and possibly won the war. France would have faced a far different army in 1939 than the one that it confronted a year later. The full force of the battle-tested Wehrmacht would be directed westward, confident that its bold new tactics would erase the shame of 1918. The French army, demoralised by months of phoney war, and having failed to appreciate the lessons of the Polish campaign, would itself suffer an ignominious defeat in May 1940.

The Bzura counter-offensive

With catastrophe looming, Rydz-Smigly began to listen more attentively to Gen Tadeusz Kutrzeba's insistent pleas to permit a counter-offensive by Army Poznan against the exposed flank of the German Eighth Army. With his original plans now appearing hopeless, Rydz-Smigly finally agreed to a counter-attack by Army Poznan. The immediate rationale for the attack was to relieve pressure on Army Lodz and permit a more orderly withdrawal to Warsaw and the Vistula. Several variants of

The German occupation of Czechoslovakia in 1939 netted the Wehrmacht a significant motor pool, including modern light tanks like the LT.35. Designated as PzKpfw 35(t) in German service, it was used by the light divisions. This picture shows a group of PzKpfw 35(t)s of Panzer Regiment 11, 1st Light Division, that took part in crushing the Bzura counter-offensive. Of the 880 casualties suffered by the division, over 600 were sustained during the intense fighting along the Bzura. (J. Magnuski)

The machine-gun armed TKS tankettes had no anti-tank capability but about 40 TK and TKS tankettes were re-armed with a 20mm anti-tank cannon. One commanded by Roman Orlik and supporting the Wolynska Cavalry Brigade during the Bzura fighting on 18 September became involved in a duel with the PzKpfw 35(t) tanks of Panzer Regiment 11, knocking out the tank of Lieutenant Victor Hohenlohe, Prinz von Ratibor. (J. Magnuski)

Kutrzeba's plan were discussed, including a delayed attack to permit the retreating Army Pomorze to join the counter-attack, but this was rejected as time was of the essence. Efforts were also planned to co-ordinate the counter-offensive with Army Lodz and units in the Warsaw area; however, the disruption to communications caused by the move of the high command to Brzesc rendered this impossible.

Although Rundstedt had long worried about the threat to his northern flank, his fears had abated as German intelligence mistakenly reported that much of Army Poznan had been transferred to Warsaw by rail. Rundstedt continued to warn Blaskowitz about the threat, but his 24th and 30th Infantry Divisions were stretched out in their march east and inattentive to the threat.

The Polish counter-attack along the Bzura River presented the Poles with a rare opportunity to enjoy modest numerical superiority over the Germans. The attack was launched with three infantry divisions – the 14th, 17th and 25th – in the centre, supported by the Podolska and Wielkopolska Cavalry Brigades on either flank. The counter-offensive started on the evening of 9 September. Although the Poles had a difficult time seizing control of the town of Piotek, reserves were thrown in, including some tankettes, and the German defence finally crumbled. By late on 10 September, both German infantry divisions were in retreat and the Poles captured over 1,500 prisoners from the 30th Infantry Division alone.

The German reaction was swift and forceful. Rather than confront the Polish attack directly, Rundstedt ordered that the opportunity be taken to encircle and destroy the Polish concentration. The 1st and 4th Panzer Divisions, already on the outskirts of Warsaw, were ordered to turn their attention westward and block any attempts by Army Poznan to slip into the capital. Within two days, the Polish attacks had bogged down and the Germans restored their numerical superiority in the area. The Polish high command ordered Kutrzeba to attack towards Radom aiming to break through and withdraw southward towards Romania. The plan was sheer fantasy. By this time, the Polish forces, which numbered nine infantry divisions and two cavalry brigades, faced 19 German divisions, five of which were Panzer and light divisions.

By far the most potent tank of the September campaign was the PzKpfw IV, armed with a short-barrelled 75mm gun. Although this type would later become the mainstay of the German tank force for most of the war, in September 1939 there were only 211 in service. (NARA)

Kutrzeba instead shifted the focus of his operations to the more realistic goal of breaking out eastward towards Warsaw via Sochaczew in concert with elements of Army Pomorze, which were arriving in the area. Kutrzeba's plan for a concentrated strike eastward was thwarted when the Germans struck first. The lack of success on the ground prompted the Wehrmacht commanders to ask for more air support. The Luftwaffe responded with a massive air attack on 16 September; 820 aircraft dropping 328,000kg (723,000lbs) of bombs. On the ground, the 16th Panzer Corps began its attacks that day as well. The units in the Bzura pocket were taking a horrible pounding from German artillery and Stukas, and Kutrzeba realised it was only a matter of time before his faltering perimeter would be ruptured. On the evening of 16 September, he ordered his units to begin taking steps to break out of the pocket through a gap north of Sochaczew, which the thinly stretched 4th Panzer Division did not control. Remnants of the Podolska and Wielkopolsa Cavalry Brigades along with the 15th and 25th Infantry Divisions broke out of the pocket and into the Kampinos Forest on the northern edge of Warsaw. The remaining Polish forces held out for two more days. Organised defence collapsed on 18 September, though it took three days before the Germans mopped up the last isolated pockets of resistance. About 120,000 Polish troops were captured and Army Pomorze and Army Poznan were wiped out.

The Bzura counter-offensive had several short-term benefits for the Polish army, giving Army Warsaw and Army Lublin time to prepare for the defence of the capital. It temporarily derailed the main German thrust towards Warsaw by about a week. German commanders writing after the war have argued that the attack would have had more serious consequences if launched earlier – as Kutrzeba himself had suggested. Polish historians have criticised the focus of the attack, arguing that it should have been launched further east, to provide a better opportunity for the armies to escape over the Vistula when the inevitable German riposte was delivered. In addition, the lack of co-ordination of the attack with the neighbouring units has been faulted.

The conduct of the Bzura counter-offensive highlights the two enormous handicaps of the Polish army in 1939 compared with the Wehrmacht. The Polish army was far less mobile than the Wehrmacht.

BZURA COUNTER-OFFENSIVE, 9–12 SEPTEMBER 1939

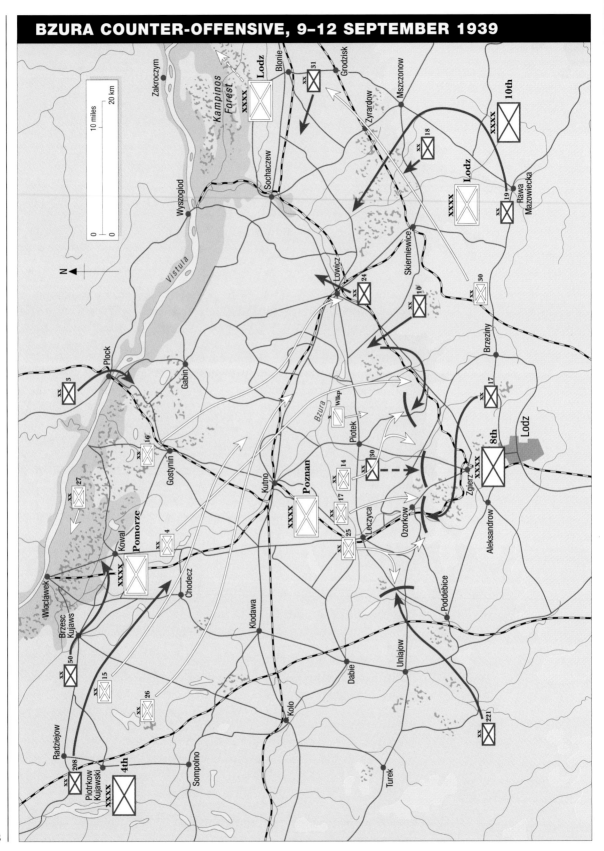

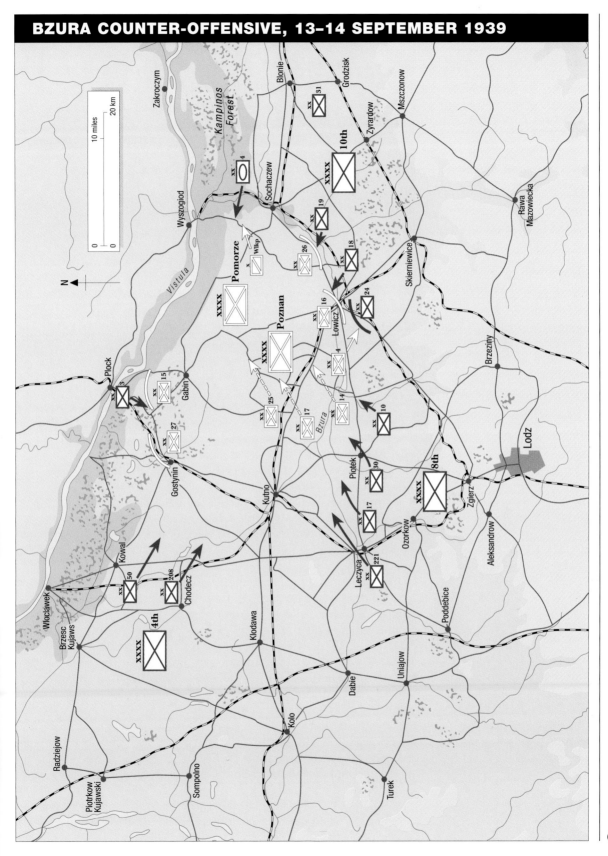

On the afternoon of 7 September 1939, elements of the 4th Panzer Division broke into the western suburbs of Warsaw. The tank units were given a bloody nose when they charged into streets covered by field guns and more infantry was brought up in support. The attack on Warsaw went on hold in a few days when the Bzura counter-offensive forced the 4th Panzer Division to turn its attention back westward. (NARA)

The Germans were able to move substantial reinforcements into the sector, some from distant locations, while the Poles desperately waited for the haggard remnants of Army Pomorze to arrive on scene. The Polish infantry fought well when the odds were near even, but the Germans were able to maintain numerical and firepower superiority by their greater tactical mobility. The second major handicap faced by the Poles was their antiquated communications. Once the counter-offensive began, Kutrzeba had little contact with Polish forces outside of his sector and was unable to co-ordinate his operations with units near Warsaw. The high command in Brzesc proved poorly suited to directing complex operations from such an isolated location.

The siege of Warsaw

The rupture between Army Lodz and Army Prusy enabled the lead elements of the German Tenth Army, the 1st and 4th Panzer Divisions, to race to the outskirts of Warsaw on the afternoon of 7 September. Polish plans for Warsaw were in flux at the time. The city was gripped in panic on the evening of 6 September when it was announced that the high command was being transferred to Brzesc and that men in selected age groups were to leave the city and form up in the area east of the capital. This last order was countermanded by the Warsaw Defence Command of General Walerian Czuma and the city's feisty mayor, Stefan Starzynski. The mayor urged Warsaw residents to remain calm and to help erect defences on the outskirts of the city. Warsaw was acting as a magnet for retreating and partially mobilised Polish units, and Polish commanders in the city decided on a prolonged defence, regardless of the plans of the high command.

German tanks from the 4th Panzer Division first began to probe into the Ochota suburbs in the early evening of 8 September but were greeted by point-blank artillery fire. The German tanks were not adequately supported by infantry and took moderate losses from camouflaged 37mm anti-tank guns and 75mm field guns that had been positioned at key street intersections. The fighting petered out later on 9 September when the 4th Panzer Division was recalled westward to help thwart the Bzura River counter-offensive.

A Polish TKS tankette company in the Warsaw area prepares for a counter-attack on 13 September 1939. These small vehicles had their occasional success against German infantry, but their thin armour and machine-gun armament gave them very limited combat power. (George Bradford)

With the counter-offensive on the Bzura checked, the German forces continued their attacks on Warsaw. Here a German infantry unit supported by a SdKfz 232 armoured car is engaged in street fighting with the Polish 17th Gnieznienska Infantry Division in the streets of Sochaczew on the approaches to Warsaw on 16 September 1939. (NARA)

When the attacks on Warsaw resumed on 15 September they came from the north, from Bock's Army Group North since Rundstedt's Army Group South was preoccupied with the Bzura fighting. Army Group North's spearhead consisted of the units of Third Army. The change in plans in mid-September had permitted Bock to deploy his forces on both sides of the Vistula, so the Third Army attack came down both the western and eastern banks of the river, hitting the Praga suburb on the east bank particularly hard. The Germans were not able to create a cordon around the city until the Bzura fighting was completed, and the second wave of fighting took place mainly in the northern suburbs. By

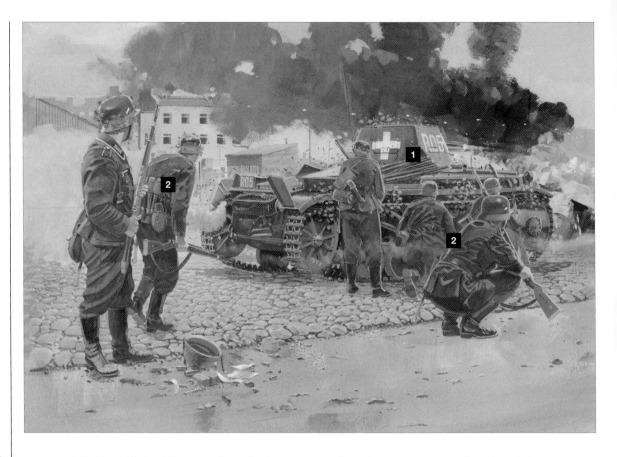

STREET FIGHTING IN WARSAW, 8 SEPTEMBER 1939
(pages 72–73)

Having suffered a bloody nose at Mokra, the 4th Panzer Division crunched through the battered Polish lines during the following two days. With the brittle Polish defences cracked wide open, the 4th Panzer Division was able to take advantage of its mobility to carry out one of the most successful Panzer missions of the campaign, exploiting its breakthrough and racing to Warsaw. Reaching the outskirts of Warsaw a week after the start of the campaign, the 4th Panzer Division pushed into the Ochota suburbs in the southwestern approaches to the city.

The ensuing battle highlighted the problems with operating mechanised forces in urban areas. By the time the 4th Panzer Division reached Ochota, the Poles had managed to scrape up a number of units to defend the capital. Lacking dedicated anti-tank weapons the Poles deployed 75mm field guns to cover key street intersections. The German Panzers of 1939 were not the impregnable steel fortresses of later years, and were vulnerable to nearly any weapon heavier than a light machine gun. They could be blown open by a 75mm field gun, and a confrontation between a Panzer blindly stumbling through unfamiliar streets and a well-placed field gun behind a barricade had predictable results and many Panzers were lost. The solution was to use infantry to locate and eliminate the field guns. But the early Panzer divisions had too few infantry for such a mission, especially when faced with Polish infantry blockaded in houses and behind barricades. Furthermore, the 4th Panzer Division had advanced so quickly that German infantry divisions were days behind.

Here, a PzKpfw II light tank (1) cautiously advances with Panzergrenadiers (2) in support. Tank-infantry cooperation in urban environments was extremely difficult as the infantry had no way to communicate with the tanks, lacking a radio link except at battalion level. The experiences of tank use in Warsaw would convince German Panzer commanders that urban battles were better left to the infantry, a lesson that still resonates with contemporary armour officers.

The attack of the 4th Panzer Division petered out after a couple of days of hard fighting due to events occurring further west. While the 4th Panzer Division had been racing to Warsaw, Gen Kutrzeba's Army Poznan had launched a surprise counterattack on German infantry divisions moving on Warsaw. The ensuing battle along the Bzura River temporarily halted the attacks on Warsaw and they did not resume until later in the month after the Polish forces were surrounded and crushed. (Howard Gerrard)

With the Pursuit Brigade out of action after the first week of air combat, air defence of Warsaw was left up to the anti-aircraft batteries. The defence mainly employed the locally manufactured Bofors 40mm gun, but 44 of these more powerful 75mm wz. 36 anti-aircraft guns were in service in 1939. (Pilsudski Institute)

20 September, the last remnants of Army Poznan had struggled into Warsaw, mainly through the Kampinos Forest north of the city.

With the fighting on the Bzura largely over by 21 September, the Wehrmacht gradually encircled the city with 13 divisions, about a third of their forces in Poland. Rundstedt's Army Group South again closed off the southern and western edges of the city. One thousand artillery pieces were brought up for the final assault. The first major attempt took place on 23 September but it made few gains as the Poles were well prepared. The next attack, on 25 September, was preceded by an enormous artillery and air bombardment, which went down in city legend as 'Black Monday'. Some 1,200 aircraft participated, even including Ju-52 transports. These tri-motors had been used as bombers during the Spanish Civil War, and were again pressed into service in this role, dropping some 13 per cent of the incendiary bombs that day. The attack led to intense clouds of smoke and dust, so bombing accuracy was poor. Indeed, so many bombs fell on German infantry in the north-western suburbs that there was a major row between army and air force commanders. The arguments were so bitter that Hitler had to personally

'Black Monday', 25 September 1939, saw the most intense German air and artillery attacks on Warsaw. Indeed the columns of smoke and dust were so dense that a significant number of bombs were dropped on German positions, causing considerable friction between the Wehrmacht and Luftwaffe over strike planning. (NARA)

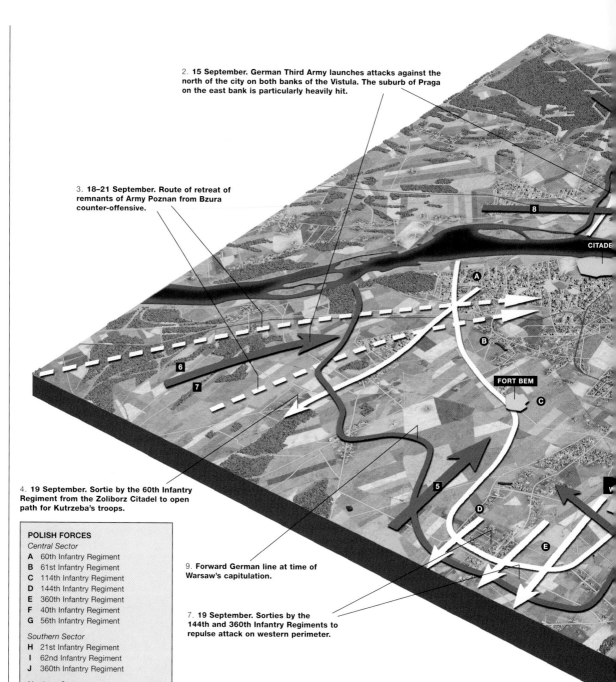

2. **15 September. German Third Army launches attacks against the north of the city on both banks of the Vistula. The suburb of Praga on the east bank is particularly heavily hit.**

3. **18–21 September. Route of retreat of remnants of Army Poznan from Bzura counter-offensive.**

8

CITADE

A

B

FORT BEM

C

6

7

5

D

4. **19 September. Sortie by the 60th Infantry Regiment from the Zoliborz Citadel to open path for Kutrzeba's troops.**

E

9. **Forward German line at time of Warsaw's capitulation.**

7. **19 September. Sorties by the 144th and 360th Infantry Regiments to repulse attack on western perimeter.**

POLISH FORCES

Central Sector
A 60th Infantry Regiment
B 61st Infantry Regiment
C 114th Infantry Regiment
D 144th Infantry Regiment
E 360th Infantry Regiment
F 40th Infantry Regiment
G 56th Infantry Regiment

Southern Sector
H 21st Infantry Regiment
I 62nd Infantry Regiment
J 360th Infantry Regiment

Northern Sector
K 79th Infantry Regiment
L 78th Infantry Regiment
M 80th Infantry Regiment
N 26th Infantry Regiment

South-east Sector
O 21st Infantry Regiment
P 136th Infantry Regiment

5. **23 September. With 1,000 artillery pieces assembled the first major attack on the city takes place. Little progress is made as the Poles are well-prepared.**

6. **25 September. 'Black Monday'; a major attack on the city is preceded by an enormous artillery and air bombardment. Some 1,200 aircraft take part in the attacks.**

THE BATTLE FOR WARSAW

8–26 September 1939, viewed from the southwest, showing the initial attacks on the city's southern suburbs by 4th Panzer Division, the retreat of the remnants of Army Poznan into the city and the subsequent German siege and assault.

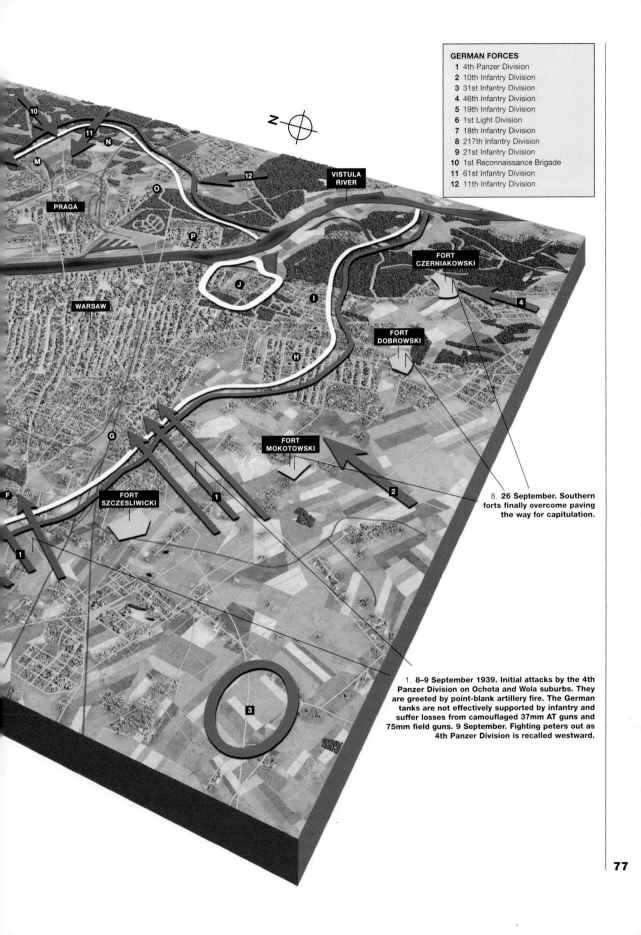

GERMAN FORCES
1 4th Panzer Division
2 10th Infantry Division
3 31st Infantry Division
4 46th Infantry Division
5 19th Infantry Division
6 1st Light Division
7 18th Infantry Division
8 217th Infantry Division
9 21st Infantry Division
10 1st Reconnaissance Brigade
11 61st Infantry Division
12 11th Infantry Division

VISTULA RIVER

PRAGA

WARSAW

FORT CZERNIAKOWSKI

FORT DOBROWSKI

FORT MOKOTOWSKI

FORT SZCZESLIWICKI

8. 26 September. Southern forts finally overcome paving the way for capitulation.

1. 8–9 September 1939. Initial attacks by the 4th Panzer Division on Ochota and Wola suburbs. They are greeted by point-blank artillery fire. The German tanks are not effectively supported by infantry and suffer losses from camouflaged 37mm AT guns and 75mm field guns. 9 September. Fighting peters out as 4th Panzer Division is recalled westward.

intervene. The expenditure of munitions surprised the Germans; the Luftwaffe used up half its supply of bombs during the Polish campaign.

Though the air attacks on 25 September were not immediately decisive, the following day German infantry finally overwhelmed the three old Tsarist forts (Forts Mokotow, Dobrowski and Czerniakow) south of the city. Hitler gave instructions to his commanders to forbid civilians to leave the city, presuming that the need for food and water would eventually force capitulation. On the evening of 26 September, the commander of Army Warsaw, General Juliusz Rommel, sent envoys to the German Eighth Army to discuss terms for surrender. Hostilities formally ended on 27 September and 140,000 Polish troops surrendered. The siege had been enormously costly with over 40,000 civilians killed, ten per cent of the buildings destroyed and about 40 per cent damaged. The nearby Modlin garrison held out until 29 September when General Wiktor Thommee surrendered his force of 24,000 troops.

THE SOVIET INVASION

Although the Polish high command had hoped to create an effective defence on the eastern bank of the Vistula, their plans were undermined before they could take effect. In the north, Army Modlin and the Special Operational Group Narew had been unable to respond to the reinforced assault out of East Prussia and, as a result, German forces were operating on the eastern bank of the Vistula in this area. Likewise, in the south, German forces had advanced over the Vistula in a number of places by the middle of the second week of the fighting.

Marshal Rydz-Smigly attempted to co-ordinate the confused situation on the east bank of the Vistula by creating two new commands on 10 September; the Northern and Southern Front. His plan took account of the geography of the area, as it was bisected by the Pripyat marshes at its centre. The Northern Front, under General S. Dab-Biernacki, was unable to create a coherent defence. Its main assignment was to prevent the German forces from penetrating southward towards Brzesc by holding a series of east-west river lines. But von Bock had committed Guderian's 19th Corps on 9 September, with an objective to cut off Polish forces attempting to form a defensive line east of the Vistula. Its 10th Panzer Division was soon plunging south towards the Bug River and the Polish high command at Brzesc. The Polish Northern Front found that its units were fighting their way through German units that had already moved south of them. By the end of 10 September, the 10th Panzer Division was south of the Biebrza River and had pinned the Suwalska Cavalry Brigade. With the Bug River having lost its potential value of holding back the advance of Bock's Army Group North, Poland's defence in the north-east was on the verge of collapse. The Germans thought that the high command was already in Lwow, little realising how close they had come to capturing the Polish supreme command.

The imminent disintegration of the Northern Front prompted Rydz-Smigly to order the withdrawal of Polish forces to the so-called Romanian bridgehead on 11 September. His intention was to preserve surviving Polish forces in the south-eastern extreme of the country until the start of the anticipated French offensive six days hence. The order showed

little recognition of reality and was more an act of desperation. The major forces west of the Vistula in central Poland were either occupied in a life-and-death struggle along the Bzura River, or in the process of retreating to the Vistula. Furthermore, the situation of the Southern Front was not as secure as Rydz-Smigly might have hoped. The German 1st Mountain Division, which had completed its arduous climb through the Carpathians, had reached Sambor that day and was on the outskirts of the regional capital of Lwow on 12 September. More ominously, the Soviet Union announced a general mobilisation on 11 September.

By 14 September, the Northern Front had been completely routed. Special Operational Group Narew existed in name only, though scattered groups continued to resist. The remnants of Army Modlin east of the Vistula succeeded in withdrawing in a more orderly fashion, but suffered heavy losses in the process. With German spearheads nearby, Rydz-Smigly and the Polish high command began withdrawing to Mlynow in the Romanian bridgehead area, and later to Kolomyja. By this stage, national co-ordination of the Polish defence effort ceased due to communication problems. The conduct of the fighting now fell on the shoulders of local commanders.

The situation with the Southern Front continued to deteriorate. The front commander, General S. Sosnkowski attempted to withdraw Army Krakow and Army Malopolska east to Lwow, but he was stymied in his attempt to co-ordinate the formations when the rapidly advancing 2nd Panzer Division and 4th Light Division drove a wedge between them. Virtually unopposed, 2nd Panzer Division had driven so deep behind Polish forces that it was able to move northward to begin the encirclement of Army Krakow. On 14 September, Army Lublin, renamed as the Central Front, began arriving from the north in a vain attempt to reinforce Army Krakow. By this stage the army was fighting a desperate battle with German forces that were closing in on three sides and which had already managed to isolate some of its units, including the 21st Mountain Division.

In the early morning of 17 September, the Polish ambassador in Moscow was informed that the Red Army was beginning to intervene in eastern Poland 'to protect its fraternal Byelorussian and Ukrainian

Although the Poles had hoped to continue the struggle by re-establishing defences on the east bank of the Vistula, the German army had already undermined any such plans by river crossings at several locations. Here, on 14 September 1939, a German infantry unit moves across a pontoon bridge erected near Tarnobrzeg. (NARA)

population'. The Polish high command, which had expected the start of the French offensive that day, was suddenly faced with an unexpected calamity. The Soviet invasion put an end to any hopes for a prolonged defence of Poland east of the Vistula.

The Soviet operations in eastern Poland had been anticipated in the secret protocols of the Molotov–Ribbentrop pact. Stalin's delay in attacking Poland was in part due to uncertainty over the reaction of the Western Allies, the unexpectedly rapid pace of the German advance, the distraction of military operations in the Far East and the time needed to mobilise the Red Army. Besides the dramatic events in Poland, Stalin was preoccupied with the undeclared war between the Soviet Union and Japan, which culminated in the decisive Soviet victory at Khalkin Gol in September 1939. An armistice was signed with Japan on 15 September, and Soviet intelligence correctly reported that German formations were already operating east of the proposed Soviet–German demarcation line. As a result, Stalin was forced to act sooner than planned.

The decapitation of the Soviet officer corps by the purges of 1937 and 1938 hindered a major military operation of this scale. The Red Army general staff estimated it needed several weeks to fully mobilise. The German advance had proceeded much more quickly than the Soviets had anticipated, forcing a hasty commitment of the ill-prepared Red Army to secure the spoils of the treaty agreement. The Red Army had expected the German operation to be an updated version of the First World War pattern: a series of border clashes until both sides mobilised and deployed their main forces for decisive battle. They had overlooked the possibility that Germany would strike from a fully mobilised posture against their smaller and only partially mobilised opponent. The planning was already well in place as the Red Army general staff had prepared plans in 1938 for intervention under various scenarios during the Munich crisis.

The Red Army was organised into two fronts and deployed no less than 25 rifle divisions, 16 cavalry divisions and 12 tank brigades with a total strength of 466,516 troops. The Red Army's tank forces sent into Poland actually exceeded the number of tanks and armoured vehicles of the Germans and Poles combined, amounting to 3,739 tanks and 380 armoured cars. The Red Air Force was also committed in strength, totalling about 2,000 combat aircraft. Fighters, consisting mainly of I-16 and I-15bis, made up about 60 per cent of the attacking force, along with medium bombers such as the SB accounting for another 30 per cent of the force. The remainder of the combat elements were army co-operation types like the R-5 biplane.

Polish defences had been stripped bare in the east. Normally the border was guarded by the Border Defence Corps (KOP) with about 18 battalions and 12,000 troops along the Soviet frontier. These forces were little more than light infantry with very little in the way of artillery support. Furthermore, many of the units had been ordered westward as reinforcements, leaving only a token force behind. The force ratio was ludicrously one-sided, roughly one Polish battalion per Soviet corps.

Red Army mobilisation was chaotic at best. Due to the upcoming harvest, it was difficult to fill out the units with their usual supply of war-mobilisation trucks from the civilian sector. As a result, Soviet formations, even tank brigades, seldom had even half of their table-of-

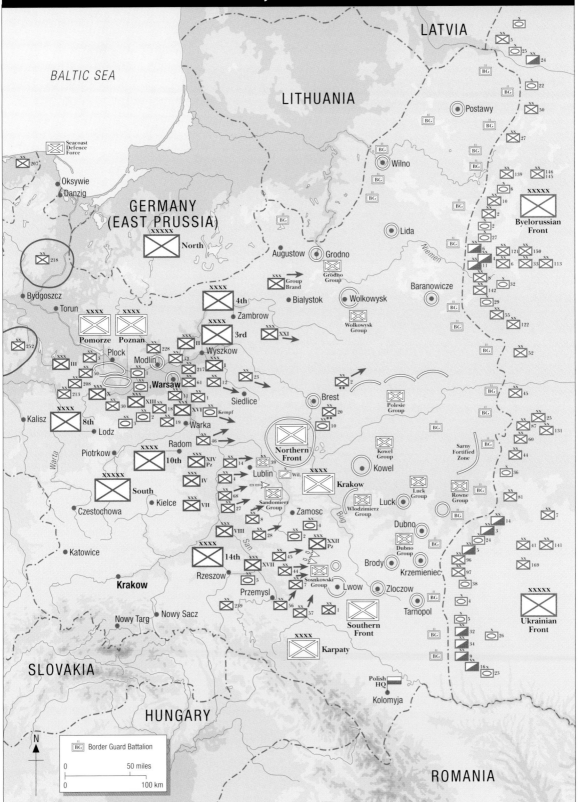

BALTIC SEA

LATVIA

LITHUANIA

GERMANY
(EAST PRUSSIA)

SLOVAKIA

HUNGARY

ROMANIA

Byelorussian
Front

Ukrainian
Front

Postawy

Wilno

Lida

Baranowicze

Augustow
Grodno
Grodno
Group
Group
Brand

Bialystok
Wolkowysk
Wolkowysk
Group

Brest

Polesie
Group

Kowel
Group

Kowel

Luck
Group

Rowne
Group

Luck

Wlodzimierz
Group

Dubno
Group

Dubno

Krzemieniec

Brody

Lwow

Zloczow

Tarnopol

Sarny
Fortified
Zone

Oksywie
Danzig

Seacoast
Defence
Force

North

Bydgoszcz

Torun

Pomorze   Poznan

Plock

Modlin

Warsaw

4th

Zambrow

3rd

Wyszkow

Siedlice

Warka

Radom

Northern
Front

Krakow

Lublin

Sosnkowski
Group

Zamosc

Lublin

Kielce

Czestochowa

Kalisz

8th

Lodz

Piotrkow

10th

South

Katowice

14th

Rzeszow

Przemysl

Krakow

Nowy Targ   Nowy Sacz

Karpaty

Southern
Front

Polish
HQ

Kolomyja

N

BG Border Guard Battalion

0   50 miles

0   100 km

The Soviet invasion on 17 September caught the Poles by surprise and little resistance was possible. Here, a Soviet BT-2 cruiser tank passes through a village in eastern Poland. The poor mechanical state of much of the mechanised equipment led to numerous breakdowns during the advance, a situation repeated in Finland in 1940 and in the opening phases of Operation Barbarossa in June 1941. (J. Magnuski)

organisation in support vehicles. There was also a shortage of spare parts for most types of vehicle including tanks. Although the Red Army order of Battle (see p.85) presents the picture of a conventionally organised force, in fact, the Soviet formations were often deployed in a haphazard fashion, loosely configured as regional groups. Indeed, there are substantial disparities in the historical records about which units participated and under which command, due to the haste under which the operation was prepared. As a result of their belated and haphazard mobilisation and the almost non-existent opposition they faced, the Red Army relied on its cavalry and armoured forces to sweep rapidly into Poland. Horse-mechanised groups were created with tank brigades supporting cavalry divisions.

There was considerable confusion on the Polish side when news of the Soviet invasion first began to filter through. At first there was some hope that the Soviets might be intervening to aid Poland, a delusion that was quickly exposed when word arrived of armed clashes. Nevertheless, the high command on the evening of 17/18 September ordered that the KOP and other units along the frontier were not to engage Soviet forces except in self-defence or if the Soviets interfered with their movement to the Romanian bridgehead. However, the order was not widely received. Instead the commander of the KOP, Brigadier-General W. Orlik-Ruckemann, ordered his troops to fight. Skirmishes between the KOP and Red Army units took place all along the frontier, especially near several of the major cities such as Wilno and Grodno, and along the fortified zone in the Sarny region. The heaviest fighting, not surprisingly, took place in Galicia in south-eastern Poland, since regular Polish army units were gravitating towards this sector near the Romanian frontier.

Galicia was one of the few areas where there was any significant aerial combat between the Polish air force and the Red Air Force. This occurred mostly on the first day of the Soviet invasion, as the surviving Polish air force units had been ordered to escape into Romania. Surviving Polish fighters had been subordinated to the Pursuit Brigade, which was headquartered near Buczacz to the south-east of Lwow. During the first contacts on 17 September, Polish fighters downed an R-5 and two SB bombers, and damaged three further Soviet aircraft. The following day the Pursuit Brigade was evacuated to Romania taking with it 35 PZL P.11 and eight PZL P.7 fighters; the last remnants of the combat elements of the Polish air force. A number of Soviet aircraft were lost in subsequent fighting, mostly to ground fire. According to recently declassified records, only five aircrew were killed during the fighting, attesting to the relatively small scale of Soviet air losses in this short campaign.

The Germans had not been forewarned about the date of the Soviet invasion and had been caught unprepared. Some German forces had already advanced beyond the boundaries set by the Molotov–Ribbentrop pact, especially Guderian's 19th Corps. On 17 September, the OKW issued a directive to its units outlining the furthest points east units could advance. On each succeeding day the OKW issued new boundary lines, gradually pulling back and preventing any encounters with the Red Army. On 20 September, Hitler explicitly ordered units to stop any combat operations east of the boundary line. All German troops were to withdraw to the definitive line laid down in the Molotov–Ribbentrop pact by 21 September. On 22 September 1939, a ceremony was held in Brzesc and the fortress was handed over to Soviet forces by the Wehrmacht. The German side was represented by the corps commander, General Heinz Guderian, while the Soviet side was represented by Colonel S.M. Krivoshein of the 29th Tank Brigade. Krivoshein was one of the Red Army's most experienced tank commanders, having commanded a Soviet tank battalion in the defence of Madrid during the Spanish Civil War. In spite of precautions there was some unintended fighting with the Red Army, especially around the city of Lwow, but generally both sides adhered to the agreement.

As a result of the intervention of the Red Army, on 17 September Rydz-Smigly ordered that all Polish units should retreat into Romania.

German troops meet the commander of a Soviet BT-7 cruiser tank in eastern Poland in late September 1939. Although there were some unintended clashes between Soviet and German forces near Lwow, relations between the two future opponents were generally proper. (J. Magnuski)

The aim was to preserve as much of the Polish army as possible and to eventually evacuate it to France to continue the struggle against the Germans. However, by this stage, only the major army groups actually received the instructions and few were in any position to act on the order. Nevertheless, the most significant tactical consequence of the Soviet intervention was to make the retention of a Romanian bridgehead impossible, thereby greatly reducing the number of Polish troops able to escape into neighbouring Romania and Hungary.

Army Krakow was one of the few remaining formations within a reasonable distance of the Romanian frontier. Fuel was collected from all available motor vehicles and provided to the army's mechanised units, including the recently formed Warsaw Mechanised Brigade and the 1st Light Tank Battalion. These tank units spearheaded the attempted break-out through the German lines near Tomaszow Lubelski on 18 September. The attack was partially successful in penetrating the lines of the 4th Light Division, but the 2nd Panzer Division counter-attacked and prevented a break-out. The attacks were repeated on 20 September and were the largest tank-versus-tank engagements of the campaign. The failure of these attacks compelled Army Krakow to surrender on 20 September 1939.

The continuing defence of Lwow by the Poles presented one of the more ticklish diplomatic situations as there were German forces on one side and Soviet on the other. Polish forces in and around the city amounted to almost six divisions. The Polish commander, General Langner, found himself completely surrounded and decided to surrender to the Red Army rather than the Germans. The Polish garrison in the city of Lwow, hemmed in by both Soviet and German forces, finally surrendered on 22 September. Ostensibly, the men would be free to go home, and the officers to find their way south to Romania. In fact the NKVD rounded up the officers before massacring them at Katyn and other locations the following year in one of the more infamous atrocities of the war.

Isolated units from the shattered Northern Front attempted to make their way through Tomaszow Lubelski but were halted by the Wehrmacht. The bulk of these forces surrendered to the Germans, but isolated units, some numbering 1,000 troops or more, continued to try to escape. The last major group, about 2,000 troops under Colonel Tadeusz Zieleniewski, surrendered near Nisko on 2 October.

The KOP border units and other scattered forces in the north had no opportunity to reach the Romanian frontier. General Franciszek Kleeberg collected about 16,000 troops under his command and intended to move westward to reinforce the Warsaw defences. Out of radio communication, they had no idea that Warsaw had fallen and they continued to push west. Encountering the German 13th Motorised Infantry Division, they fought a four-day battle around Kock before finally surrendering on 6 October 1939.

In spite of the puny size of Polish forces in the border area, the Red Army lost 996 men and 2,383 wounded in the fighting. Tank casualties amounted to 42 combat losses and a further 429 mechanical breakdowns and other non-combat losses.

The Soviet invasion shortened the Polish campaign by several weeks. The eastern region of Poland was less developed than the western areas. It also had fewer roads and the terrain was more suitable for defence. As

RED ARMY ORDER OF BATTLE, 17 SEPTEMBER 1939

Byelorussian Front – Komandarm Mikhail P. Kovalev
3rd Army – Komkor Vasily I. Kuznetsov
  4th Rifle Corps
    27th Rifle Division
    50th Rifle Division
  Lepel Group
    5th Rifle Division
    24th Cavalry Division
    22nd Tank Brigade
    25th Tank Brigade
11th Army – Komkor Nikifor Medvedev
  16th Rifle Corps
    2nd Rifle Division
    100th Rifle Division
  3rd Cavalry Corps
    7th Cavalry Division
    36th Cavalry Division
    6th Tank Brigade
  24th Rifle Corps (Reserve)
    139th Rifle Division
    145th Rifle Division
10th Army – Komkor I.G. Zakharin
  11th Rifle Corps
    6th Rifle Division
    33rd Rifle Division
    121st Rifle Division
  16th Rifle Corps
    8th Rifle Division
    52nd Rifle Division
    55th Rifle Division
  3rd Rifle Corps (Reserve)
    113th Rifle Division
    33rd Rifle Division
Dzherzhinsk Cavalry Mechanised Group – Komkor I.V. Boldin
  6th Cavalry Corps
    4th Cavalry Division
    6th Cavalry Division
    11th Cavalry Division
  5th Rifle Corps
    4th Rifle Division
    13th Rifle Division
  15th Tank Corps
    2nd Tank Brigade
    20th Motorised Brigade
    21st Tank Brigade
    27th Tank Brigade

4th Army – Komdiv Vasily Chuikov
  23rd Rifle Corps
    93rd Rifle Division
    109th Rifle Division
    152nd Rifle Division
  29th Tank Brigade
  32nd Tank Brigade

Ukrainian Front – Komandarm Semyon Timoshenko
5th Army – Komdiv Ivan Sovietnikov
  8th Rifle Corps
    81st Rifle Division
    44th Rifle Division
    14th Rifle Division
  15th Rifle Corps
    87th Rifle Division
    45th Rifle Division
  36th Tank Brigade
6th Army – Komkor Filipp Golikov
  2nd Cavalry Corps
    3rd Cavalry Division
    14th Cavalry Division
    24th Tank Brigade
  17th Rifle Corps
    96th Rifle Division
    97th Rifle Division
  38th Tank Brigade
  10th Tank Brigade
12th Army – Komandarm Ivan Tyuleniev
  13th Rifle Corps
    72nd Rifle Division
    99th Rifle Division
  4th Cavalry Corps
    32nd Cavalry Division
    34th Cavalry Division
  26th Tank Brigade
  5th Cavalry Corps
    9th Cavalry Division
    16th Cavalry Division
  23rd Tank Brigade
  25th Tank Corps
    1st Motorised Brigade
    4th Tank Brigade
    5th Tank Brigade
  13th Independent Rifle Corps
    72nd Rifle Division
    146th Rifle Division
    124th Rifle Division
Front Reserve
  36th Rifle Corps
    25th Rifle Division
    7th Rifle Division
    131st Rifle Division

Rundstedt pointed out, German casualties in the second two weeks of fighting were heavier than in the first two weeks of the war as the scale and intensity of the fighting escalated. The immediate tactical consequence for the Polish army was to prevent a large portion of the forces who had retreated eastward from reaching Romania. The Red Army had captured 99,149 Polish troops by 2 October 1939. Later records state that they eventually captured 452,536 Polish troops, but this number included a significant number of government officials, postal workers, police and other non-military personnel who were rounded up as part of the policy to 'de-Polonize' the region. Most of the officers captured in 1939 were murdered in 1940 at Katyn and other locations, while many of the troops were deported to Siberia along with thousands of government officials, civic leaders, teachers and clergy.

CONCLUSION

Polish casualties in the 1939 campaign amounted to about 66,300 dead, 133,700 wounded, 587,000 prisoners captured by Germany and over 100,000 by the Soviet Union. German casualties were about 16,000 dead and 32,000 wounded. A total of 674 German tanks were knocked out, of which 217 were total write-offs. The 4th Panzer Division suffered the heaviest tank losses, a total of 81 tanks, due to its tangle with the cavalry at Mokra and its ill-fated dash into the Warsaw suburbs. Other equipment losses included 319 armoured cars, 195 artillery pieces, 6,046 vehicles and 5,538 motorcycles.

For the German army, the Polish campaign was a vital learning experience prior to its more daunting mission against its First World War adversary, France. Today it is difficult to recall how highly regarded the French army was in 1939. It was a large, well-equipped force with a modern arsenal and a heritage of victory in the 1914–18 war. It was only after the French defeat in 1940 that its underlying shortcomings became evident. For the German army, the Polish campaign was a necessary test of men and machines. The outcome of the contest was never in serious doubt, but new tactics, training and technology had to be proven. The fighting highlighted the skills of the better commanders and troops while also providing many German divisions with their first combat experience. It was especially valuable in validating the Panzer divisions and the revolutionary potential of combined arms warfare. Some French and British observers dismissed the outcome of the campaign as inevitable due to the poor performance of the Polish army, thereby underestimating the importance of the new tactics. The Germans were

The Polish 10th Mechanised Brigade, nicknamed the Black Brigade because of their black leather tanker's jackets, was one of the units that withdrew into Romania and Hungary in late September. Commanded by Stanislaw Maczek, seen in the centre of the photo in the beret, the unit was re-formed twice, in France in 1940 and again in Britain in the same year. It became the core of the 1st Polish Armoured Division, famous for its role in the Falaise Gap fighting in Normandy in 1944. (J. Magnuski)

German motorcycle reconnaissance units ranged deep behind Polish lines, but as a result were vulnerable to ambush. More motorcycles were lost during the campaign than any other type of motor vehicle. This is a civilian motorcycle pressed into service. The riders wear an older pattern German stalhelm, still seen in 1939 in some reserve units and in units that had recently been formed until enough of the new pattern helmet were available. (NARA)

not so dismissive of Polish performance in 1939, recognising that the intensity of the fighting verified the new tactical doctrine. More perceptive British observers dubbed the new combined arms tactics as 'Blitzkrieg', a word that entered the military vocabulary a few months later following the stunning defeat of France.

While German army performance in Poland had been very good, the campaign had revealed shortcomings that needed to be addressed. The light divisions had proven to be a failure, lacking the strength of the infantry divisions or the firepower of the Panzer divisions. In view of the success of the Panzer divisions, the light divisions were converted to this pattern in time for the French campaign. The Polish fighting revealed the need to improve many aspects of combined arms operations. The Panzer divisions were tank heavy and infantry light. Tank and infantry co-operation at the beginning of the war was poor, as was so evident at

Some of the most confused fighting of the campaign took place around the city of Lwow after the German and Soviet forces became entangled in a number of clashes. The Poles began negotiating a surrender with the Germans on 21 September, seen here under a flag of truce with an officer from one of the German mountain divisions. (NARA)

battles like Mokra, and it needed attention. The Luftwaffe had played an important role in the campaign, gaining air superiority and conducting interdiction missions, but greater consideration had to be paid to co-ordinating air operations with ground forces.

The Red Army, concentrating on its victory over Japan at Khalkin Gol in the same period, learned some lessons from the Polish experience but ignored most others. The level of training of all ranks was poor, with particular weaknesses in the senior officer ranks and among specialised troops. German officers who had previous contact with the Red Army through joint training in the late 1920s were surprised at how badly the Red Army had deteriorated by 1939. Halder concluded that it would take them a decade to return to the level of competence of the early 1930s prior to the purges. The scale of tank losses was indicative of this decline. Almost 15 per cent of the Red Army's tank force was lost during two weeks of operations against a token opponent. These losses came because the Red Army was ill-prepared to operate sophisticated equipment in battlefield conditions. It was a scenario that would become all the more evident a few months later during the invasion of Finland, where the Red Army's pervasive problems were much more clearly revealed to the world. For the German commanders, the Polish campaign suggested that in spite of their shiny new technology, the Red Army was a mere paper tiger. The Finnish war three months later confirmed suspicions and provided a further enticement for Hitler's war plans in the east.

A total of about 100,000 Polish troops escaped into Romania, Hungary and the Baltic republics in 1939. These men were gradually spirited out and about 35,000 made their way to France where they served in four infantry divisions and a mechanised brigade during the 1940 campaign. After the defeat of France, about 19,000 of these troops made their way to Britain and North Africa, where they formed the seed of yet another Polish army. At the core of the group was the remnants of Colonel Stanislaw Maczek's 10th Mechanised Brigade, which had performed so well with Army Krakow in 1939. Maczek later commanded the mechanised brigade in France in 1940 and, after the evacuation to Britain, he organised the 1st Polish Armoured Division, which fought under his command in 1944–45. The 1st Polish Armoured Division is

most famous for its role in closing the Falaise Gap in the Normandy campaign. The Polish Second Corps was created in the Mediterranean by Polish survivors of the Soviet prisoner-of-war camps, released by Stalin starting in 1942. These units, who won fame for their capture of Monte Cassino in 1944, took part in the later stages of the Italian campaign.

If the Polish campaign had revealed the technical excellence of the Wehrmacht, it also began to reveal its dark side. While civilian casualties in war are ubiquitous, the scale and brutality of German reprisals in Poland in 1939 were unusually savage. The worst atrocities were committed by German paramilitary formations and the new SS units. Indeed, the actions of the SS led some Wehrmacht commanders such as Blaskowitz to complain directly to Hitler. These were only hints of far worse to come, as warfare in eastern Europe would degenerate into appalling savagery in the later years of the war.

For Poland, the Second World War was an unredeemed tragedy. During the war, one in six Poles died due to the brutal occupation policies of the Nazi and Soviet regimes. Europe's most thriving Jewish community was annihilated, and the names of the German death camps in Poland such as Auschwitz, Belzec and Treblinka have become synonyms for genocide. The Allied victory in 1945 offered little solace, as Poland was subjected to nearly 50 years of communist rule imposed by the Soviet Union. Memories of the valiant defence in 1939 have offered small compensation compared with the tragedy that ensued.

The consequences of the Polish campaign continued to be felt for decades afterwards. In spite of being nominally allied to Poland after the German invasion of 1941, Stalin insisted that the Soviet Union be allowed to keep the half of Poland it seized in 1939. In compensation, Poland was allotted territory in eastern Germany. Instead of gaining 'living space' in the east, Germany contracted; East Prussia disappeared and the German populations in the east were forcibly displaced. In swallowing western Ukraine, the Soviet Union contributed to its own demise. Western Ukraine has long been the well-spring of Ukrainian nationalism and during the crisis of 1991, Ukrainian agitation for statehood was one of the catalysts for the dissolution of the Soviet Union.

THE BATTLEFIELD TODAY

Tracing the September 1939 campaign in Poland today is complicated by geography, history and politics. Poland's borders shifted dramatically during the Second World War. The eastern half of the old Polish republic was taken over by the Soviet Union in 1939 and it remained in Soviet hands until the collapse of the USSR in 1991. Now, these territories are part of the newly independent countries of Belarus, Ukraine and Lithuania. Since Poland and the Soviet Union were nominally allies from 1941 to 1945, Stalin suggested that Poland be compensated for the loss of its territory with German territory. As a result, Poland shifted westward, with Berlin now nearer the Polish border. East Prussia no longer exists, having been absorbed by Poland except for the city of Koenigsberg (now the Russian city of Kaliningrad). As a result, the former borders of 1939 Poland are difficult to trace without a good map of the period.

The Polish campaign lives on in Poland in film and print. Poland's premier film director, Andrzej Wajda, based his 1959 film *Lotna* around the quixotic bravery of a doomed cavalry unit. His surrealistic depiction of the cavalry attacking tanks helped cement this myth into Polish legend. (Film Polski)

Tracing sites of the 1939 battles is further hindered by later history and politics. Poland was a battleground on several later occasions during the Second World War, and so the 1939 campaign competes with other commemorations. Poland's former eastern provinces were the site of the opening phase of Operation Barbarossa in June 1941. In 1944 the Red Army swept through eastern Poland in the wake of Operation Bagration, ending up along the eastern banks of the Vistula. Warsaw was the most severely damaged of Poland's cities. The Jewish quarter of the capital was razed in the wake of the Warsaw ghetto uprising of April 1943, while the rest of the city was systematically destroyed by German engineer troops as a reprisal against the city-wide Warsaw Uprising of August 1944. When the Red Army marched into the city in January 1945, there was nothing but ruins. As a result, Warsaw has been rebuilt from scratch since the war, and its Old City is a reconstruction. The old royal capital of Krakow miraculously escaped extensive war damage, but it did not figure prominently in the 1939 fighting. Danzig, now Gdansk, was also severely damaged during the 1945 fighting. It still retains the flavour of a German Baltic port.

The communist government, which took power in Poland after the war, favoured the commemoration of battles by the Polish People's Army (LWP), which fought alongside the Red Army from 1944 to 1945. The prewar Polish army was regarded, at least by the government, as the tool of the old bourgeois regime. In this climate battlefields like Studzianki, site of the 1944 Vistula River crossing, were amply preserved, while other battlefields from 1939 were either ignored or received minimal attention.

A number of artefacts of the September campaign have been preserved in Poland, including the sole surviving example of the PZL P.11c fighter, on display at the aviation museum in Krakow. No examples of either the P.23 *Karas* or P.37 *Los* have survived. (Author)

There were some exceptions to this, notably the preservation of the Westerplatte garrison. In spite of the tendentious attitude of the government, the Poles' fascination with their military history meant that the memories could not be totally ignored. Other monuments were created due to local initiatives. The postwar Polish army did not share the politicians' viewpoint and sponsored many studies of the 1939 campaign.

The collapse of communism in Poland in the 1980s has had the paradoxical effect of giving the Poles the opportunity to freely study their past history and to freely ignore it. The political and economic turmoil of the 1990s has prevented any extensive government expenditure on historical preservation, though there have been many local initiatives. At the national level, the armed forces museum in Warsaw now has a more comprehensive exhibit on the 1939 campaign than was possible during the communist period. Unfortunately, after the devastation of German and Soviet occupation and a half-century of neglect, the artefacts of war are few. The museum has no example of a Polish armoured vehicle from the war, while combat aircraft are limited to a single P.11 fighter preserved in Krakow. There are larger collections of small arms and some artillery. The German army captured large quantities of Polish equipment after 1939, so Polish equipment has shown up in a surprisingly wide variety of locations. A partial TKS tankette was recovered in Sweden, having been used by German units in neighbouring Finland during the war. The Yugoslav army museum in Belgrade had an ex-German TK tankette on display for many years, though its status at the moment is not clear given the recent conflicts in the Balkans. A C2P artillery tractor turned up on the Franco-Spanish border and was preserved in a private collection in Belgium. Some Polish aircraft from the 1939 period that were exported prior to the war are in foreign collections. Polish small arms are widely found in international military museums. For example, the US Army's Ordnance Museum at Aberdeen Proving Ground has two examples of the 46mm infantry mortar, the 7.92mm anti-tank rifle and other rifles and pistols that were captured by the US Army from the Wehrmacht in 1944–45. The Soviet Union also captured a considerable amount of Polish equipment in 1939 but little of it has been preserved. The sole surviving 7TP tank was scrapped, but the central armour museum at Kubinka outside Moscow still has a Polish TKS tankette and a Renault R-35, which is probably the example captured from the 21st Tank Battalion in 1939. No Polish aircraft are known to survive in former Soviet collections.

Due to the de-Nazification of Germany after the war and widespread anti-war sentiment, there has been little government effort in Germany to preserve artefacts from the war except for documents and photographs. There are few surviving German items that can be directly linked to the 1939 campaign. It is possible that some preserved armoured vehicles took part in the Polish campaign, such as the PzKpfw 35(t) preserved at the Ordnance Museum at Aberdeen Proving Grounds in the United States. However, few early German armoured vehicles have survived the war, and the same is the case for 1939-period aircraft.

Concrete bunkers tend to survive longer than other military artefacts and this has been the case with the 1939 campaign. A significant number of 1939-era defensive works are still intact, though access is hampered in some cases due to their location on military bases or private land. There are a number of bunkers still intact around Mlawa. The fortified garrison of Modlin can also be visited. A number of the forts around Warsaw have survived, and the Polish army museum is converting one of them into an armoured vehicle museum. Some effort is needed to find fortifications not only due to their dispersion in the countryside but also because of the steady accretion of foreign fortifications in Poland over the centuries, which often makes the exercise quite confusing. The German army built a number of bunker complexes in Poland after 1939 that might be confused with the earlier Polish bunkers. There are even a few Soviet bunkers of the Stalin line built in 1940–41 near Przemysl. Fortunately, there has been a resurgence in interest in military architecture in Poland in the past decade, which has resulted in many fine books and journals such as the magazine *Forteca*. These publications are an excellent aid in tracking down specific examples of fortifications.

Much of the documentation on the 1939 campaign has been lost over the years due to the destruction of the Polish military archives by the Germans during the 1939–44 occupation and the destruction of much of the German military archives during the later years of the war. Still, much has been preserved and can be found in major military archives such as Freiburg in Germany and Rembertow in Poland. There are also some significant archives outside of Germany and Poland. Many of the Polish soldiers who escaped in 1939 made their way to Britain where they were re-formed into new units that fought alongside the Allies for the remainder of the war. Their records are preserved at the Sikorski Institute near Hyde Park in London, which also has a collection of uniforms from the 1939 period. Other Polish archives were formed abroad, such as the Pilsudski Institute in New York, which has also preserved prewar and wartime records.

The 1939 campaign has been the subject of a number of documentaries and films. One of the first was the German propaganda film *Kampfgeschwader Lutzow*, a pseudo-documentary on the war that includes staged footage of a Polish cavalry charge against tanks. This film occasionally reappears in television documentaries as authentic footage. For political reasons, Polish films about the 1939 campaign were not favoured during the communist years, though there were some important exceptions. Poland's premier film director, Andrzej Wajda, grew up in a cavalry garrison in eastern Poland before the war. His 1959 film *Lotna*, about a cursed horse and the fate of its doomed cavalry troop in 1939, was an epitaph to prewar Poland. Its surrealistic imagery of a cavalry charge against tanks helped enshrine this myth in Polish national legend, becoming a symbol of the brave but doomed struggle of 1939.

FURTHER READING

Since the campaign in Poland started the Second World War, there is a considerable volume of literature in English on the political and diplomatic events leading up to the war. These works tend to focus on the great powers, though there have been several recent studies on Poland's diplomatic actions by Anita Prazmowska, published in Britain. English-language coverage of the military actions in Poland is very thin; the best known is the Kennedy study listed below, which was prepared for the US Army in the 1950s. It remains a very useful account, though it is weak on the Polish side and has a number of glaring errors, such as its widely repeated statement that the Polish air force was destroyed on the ground on 1 September.

Of the major combatants, the Polish side of the 1939 campaign is best covered in the available literature. However, this is not immediately accessible to an English-language audience, since nearly all of the relevant publications are in Polish. The 1939 campaign was a seminal event in recent Polish history, and military history is a popular subject for the general audience. Due to Polish exposure to the Soviet analytic tradition during the Cold War, several of the broad surveys published in Poland in the 1970s and 1980s are of particularly high quality with a strong grounding in modern tactical and operational doctrine, offering pungent analysis of the campaign. For political reasons, these works were excessively critical of the 1939 leadership. They were prepared with official encouragement and published by the Ministry of Defence publishing house, WMON, in Warsaw. Examples include the multi-author *Polski czyn zbrojny w II wojnie swiatowej: Wojna obronna Polski 1939*, published in 1979, and Tadeusz Jurga's numerous works on the subject. Other seminal works were E. Kozlowski's *Wojsko Polskie 1936–1939*, published in 1974, on the Polish army's modernisation programme of 1936, and Marian Zgorniak's *Sytuacja militarna Europy w okresie kryzysu politicznego 1938r*, published in 1979 on the military situation in Europe during the Czech crisis.

There are other important studies on the war, far too numerous to mention. Indeed, there is a Polish bibliography on the war that lists thousands of titles on the 1939 campaign. Besides the full-length books, there has been excellent coverage of more specialised aspects the 1939 campaign in the Polish military history journal *Wojskowy przeglad historyczne*. Polish publications cover a broad range of subjects and include fairly comprehensive selection of unit histories, army group histories, histories of the combat arms (especially the cavalry), armoured force, air force and navy, and technical histories of the weapons and equipment.

The main problem with accounts published in Poland prior to 1989 is the political sensitivity of the Soviet invasion of 17 September. Fortunately, the problem has disappeared since the fall of the communist government, and there has been more balanced coverage of the Soviet role since then, both from Polish and Russian sources. Besides the extensive literature published in Poland, there has been important work published by officers from the Polish forces who escaped to Britain in 1940. The Sikorski Institute in London has published an essential multi-volume history of the campaign. There have also been numerous specialist publications that amplify the material published in Poland. The émigré literature helped cover forbidden subjects during the years of communist rule in Poland, such as the publication of Karol Liszewski's *Wojna polsko–sowiecka 1939* (The Polish–Soviet War of 1939) by the Polish Cultural Foundation in London in 1986.

English-language accounts of the Polish aspects of the campaign are much less extensive. There is excellent coverage on subjects popular to military enthusiasts, especially aircraft and air force. There is also some important scholarly work in diplomatic history, but very little on military policy. For those wishing to find more detail on the Polish cavalry in 1939, the author wrote a more in-depth article, 'Polish Cavalry against the Panzers', which appeared in the January/February 1984 issue of *Armour* magazine.

German literature on the campaign is less extensive than the Polish, as the 1939 war was a less important event in modern German military history than later campaigns. One of the better recent accounts was Janusz Piekalkiewicz's *Polen Feldzug: Hitler und Stalin zerschlagen die Polnische Republik*, published in 1982. A very useful source is the reprint of the German general staff daily situation maps for the campaign: Klaus-Jurgen Thies, *Der Zweite Weltkrieg im Kartenbild: Band 1 Der Polenfeldzug*, published by Biblio Verlag in 1989. The Polish campaign is mentioned in the many memoirs, unit histories and surveys of the war, but there are fewer specialised monographs than in Polish. There is extensive coverage of German aircraft, weapons and uniforms of the 1939 campaign in the enthusiast literature on the war in English.

The Soviet invasion of Poland in 1939 was a non-event in Russian military literature through the Cold War years so as not to aggravate already sensitive Polish–Soviet relations. During the Khrushchev thaw, some memoirs included references to the 'liberation of western Byelorussia and Ukraine in 1939', but there was little detail. The subject has been taken off the forbidden list since 1991, but the literature is still slim due to the near collapse of the publishing of serious histories of the Second World War. Polish researchers took advantage of the short-lived window of opportunity in the Russian archives in the early 1990s to extract many documents, which have been published in a number of collections in Polish, both in book form and in scholarly journals. One of the few new campaign studies to have resulted from this archival work was Janusz Magnuski and Maksim Kolomiets' book on Soviet armoured operations in Poland in 1939, *Czerwony Blitzkrieg* (Red Blitzkrieg) published in 1994 in Poland.

Due to the language barriers presented by Polish, German and Russian sources, the books listed here are limited to English accounts.

Bethell, Nicholas, *The War Hitler Won: The Fall of Poland September 1939* (Holt, Rinehart, Winston, 1972). An examination of the conflict from the perspective of British diplomacy during the period.

Citino, Robert, *The Evolution of Blitzkrieg Tactics: Germany Defends Itself Against Poland 1918–1933* (Greenwood, 1987). This is a short academic history of German war preparations in the event of conflict with Poland during the Weimar Republic.

Corum, James, *The Roots of Blitzkrieg: Hans von Seeckt and German Military Reform* (University of Kansas, 1992). An excellent study of the underpinnings of German combined arms warfare covering the years immediately after the First World War.

Cynk, Jerzy B., *History of the Polish Air Force 1918–1968* (Osprey, 1972) This remains the best single volume on Polish combat operations in 1939 published in English, though the newer Belcarz and Peczkowski book *White Eagles* provides more detail.

Hooton, E.R., *Phoenix Triumphant: The Rise and Rise of the Luftwaffe* (Arms & Armour 1994). An excellent overview of Luftwaffe operations in the early years of the war including the 1939 Polish campaign.

Kennedy, Robert, *The German Campaign in Poland 1939* (US Army Pamphlet 20-255, 1956). A US army study that remains the best account in English of the German aspects of the campaign.

Kliment, Charles, and Nakladal, B., *Germany's First Ally: Armed Forces of the Slovak State 1939–45* (Schiffer, 1997). A detailed account of the Slovak army during the war, including its participation in the Polish campaign.

Maier, Klaus, et. al., *Germany and the Second World War, Vol. 2: Germany's Initial Conquests in Europe* (Oxford, 1991). This is a semi-official history of the war by the German Military History Institute in Freiburg. The account of the military operations in Poland is surprisingly mediocre, but the other chapters are valuable in placing the campaign within the broader perspective of German war plans.

May, Ernest, *Strange Victory: Hitler's Conquest of France* (Hill & Wang, 2001). An intriguing new account of French war planning and the consequences of Gamelin's policies in 1939.

Norwid-Neugebauer, M., *The Defence of Poland: September 1939* (Kolin Ltd, 1940). This excellent, but little-known account published in the United Kingdom in 1940 provides the perspective of a Polish general on the conduct of the campaign.

Sword, Keith (ed.), *The Soviet Takeover of the Polish Eastern Provinces 1939-41* (University of London, 1989). Although concerned mainly with Soviet occupation policy, this book contains two of the best essays available in English on the Soviet invasion and the Polish military response.

Peszke, Michael A., *The Polish Navy 1939–1945* (Hippocrene, 1999). A recent account on the Polish navy in the Second World War.

Zaloga, S., *The Polish Army 1939–45* (Osprey Men-at-Arms 117, 1982). A more detailed look at Polish uniforms and equipment in the 1939 campaign and the fate of the army later in the war.

Zaloga, S., and Madej, V., *The Polish Campaign 1939* (Hippocrene, 1985). A detailed look at the organisation, doctrine and equipment of the Polish army in 1939.

INDEX

Figures in **bold** refer to illustrations